PHILOSOPHY IN AMERICA
AN AMS REPRINT SERIES

JONATHAN EDWARDS

A RETROSPECT

AMS PRESS

NEW YORK

Library of Congress Cataloging in Publication Data

Gardiner, Harry Norman, 1855-1927, ed.
  Jonathan Edwards, a retrospect.

  (Philosophy in America)
  Reprint of the 1901 ed. published by Houghton,
Mifflin, Boston.
  1. Edwards, Jonathan, 1703-1758—Addresses, essays,
lectures.   I. Title.
BX7260.E3G3   1980   285.8'092'4   75-3133
ISBN 0-404-59142-6

Reprinted from the edition of 1902, Boston. [Trim size of the original has been slightly altered in this edition. Original: 12.3 × 18.7
cm. Text area of the original remains the same].

JONATHAN EDWARDS

A RETROSPECT

BEING THE ADDRESSES DELIVERED
IN CONNECTION WITH THE UNVEILING OF A MEMORIAL
IN THE FIRST CHURCH OF CHRIST IN NORTHAMPTON
MASSACHUSETTS ON THE ONE HUNDRED AND
FIFTIETH ANNIVERSARY OF HIS
DISMISSAL FROM THE PASTORATE
OF THAT CHURCH

EDITED BY

H. NORMAN GARDINER

Professor of Philosophy in Smith College,
Chairman of the Edwards
Memorial Committee

BOSTON AND NEW YORK
HOUGHTON, MIFFLIN AND COMPANY
The Riverside Press, Cambridge
1901

CONTENTS

Jonathan Edwards.

INTRODUCTION

JONATHAN EDWARDS was dismissed from
the pastorate of the First Church of Christ
in Northampton, Mass., on Friday the 22d
of June, 1750. The dismissal was regular
in form, in accordance with the usual methods of Congregational procedure, and, but
for the attendant circumstances, would give
little occasion for comment. In fact, it was
a public rejection and banishment. This
treatment of Edwards, recognized even then
as the most eminent divine in New England,
regarded now as among the world's immor-
tals, has long been, and probably will long
continue to be, a source of reproach to his
church and people. It was, indeed, a most
lamentable ending of an illustrious ministry,
a sadly pathetic recompense for the laborious
and fruitful service of twenty-three years.
No apology can atone for the hatred, malice,
and all uncharitableness which characterized
to so large an extent the opposition to him,
though the later contrite and public confes-

sion of its leading spirit may seem to some
to go a long way in this direction. But in
the course of time the quality in the affairs
of men is apt to change somewhat in appearance. Particular features of an event lose,
while others gain in importance, and the
whole is seen in a new set of relations in new
light. This is true of Edwards' banishment
from Northampton. Without derogating in
any way from the clear intellectual superior-
ity and the lofty dignity of the character
displayed by him in the long and painful
controversy which ended in his dismissal, and
without at all glossing over the passion and
prejudice in the proceedings against him, it
is now possible perhaps to do something like
justice to both sides, to see that the right
was not wholly with the one, nor the wrong
wholly with the other, to understand better
than heretofore both the motives and the consequences of this event, and to find in it the
operation of profounder spiritual forces than
appear if we view it merely as the tragedy
of an individual life or as a regrettable epi-
sode in the annals of a particular church.
Edwards was so great, so representative, so
influential, that his fate exhibits an historic

situation, a situation which he more than
any other man had created, a conflict and a
crisis in the religious life of New England.
And the situation and the man alike require
their interpretation from the broader historical point of view.

A unique opportunity was afforded for an
attempt at appreciation from this broader
point of view by the unveiling of a Memorial
to Edwards in the First Church in Northampton on Friday the 22d of June, 1900, just a
hundred and fifty years after his dismissal.
This is not the only memorial of Edwards in
Northampton.   In spite of its ancient quarrel, the town has never been wanting in regard for its greatest inhabitant.   The noble
elm which tradition says he planted is still
reverently preserved on the site of his dwelling and protected, as far as possible, from
the ravages of time.   Near the grave of his
friend David Brainerd in the old burying-
ground a citizen of the town years ago
erected a stone inscribed to the memory of
" The American Theologian," and of his
Scotch admirer, Dr. Chalmers.   Not far off,
by one of the gateways, a granite monument
contains the names of Jonathan Edwards,

his wife, and all their children side by side
with one of a similar character recording
the names of his son-in-law, Timothy Dwight,
his wife, and their children. Worthiest of
all tributes to his memory, erected not merely
to perpetuate his name, but to continue the
supreme work of his life, the promotion in
varied forms of Christian service of the glory
of God in the salvation of men, is the Edwards Church, founded in 1833, a daughter
of the First Church, and one of the most
flourishing of the religious societies of the
town. The Memorial now placed in the
First Church is a bronze tablet, set in a
massive frame of green-stained oak, and containing a two-thirds length relief figure of
Edwards, life size or larger, represented as
if preaching. On the panel beneath the
figure is the simple inscription : —

IN MEMORY OF

JONATHAN EDWARDS

MINISTER OF NORTHAMPTON

FROM FEBRUARY 15 1727 TO JUNE 22 1750

THE LAW OF TRUTH WAS IN HIS MOUTH AND

UNRIGHTEOUSNESS WAS NOT FOUND IN HIS LIPS

HE WALKED WITH ME IN PEACE AND UPRIGHTNESS

AND DID TURN MANY AWAY FROM INIQUITY

MAL. 2 : 6.

The tablet was erected under authorization of the parish, but the cost was defrayed by public subscription. The Memorial, therefore, represents neither the contrition nor the pride of the local church, but rather a widely spread, and to a certain extent newly awakened regard for the genius and character of its subject and a sympathetic interest in what appealed to many as a simple act of historic justice.[1]

The commemorative exercises were attended by a representative assembly of townspeople and visitors, including not a few of the theologian's descendants, together with pastors of neighboring churches and delegates from the churches which a century and a half before had pronounced the dissolution of the pastoral relations, and from the church in Stockbridge to which Edwards ministered while missionary to the Indians after his banishment from Northampton.[2]

[1] The tablet was designed and sculptured by Herbert Adams, with the assistance of Vincent C. Griffith for the architectural features, and was cast by the *cire perdue* process at the Roman Bronze Works, New York. The total dimensions are about eight feet by five. It is placed in the church in the middle space of the east wall, holding a commanding position.

[2] The churches composing the council were those of En-

Greetings were received by letter from the
church which bears his name on the West-
ern plains, the Edwards Church of Daven-
port, Iowa, and from not a few distinguished
scholars, admirers of his character and writings, in this country and abroad.   Yale, the
college where he graduated, where he taught,
and from which he was summoned to the
ministry in Northampton and Princeton University, of which, then Nassau Hall, the College of New Jersey, he was the president
when he died, sent special greetings by chosen
representatives.   The Rev. Professor George
P. Fisher, D. D., spoke for the former, Professor Alexander T. Ormond, Ph. D., for the
latter.   After an organ voluntary, prayer
was offered by the Rev. Peter McMillan,
pastor of the Edwards Church in Northampton.   The Rev. Dr. Henry T. Rose, pastor
of the First Church, gave the address of wel-

field, Sheffield, Sutton, Reading (now Wakefield), Sunder-
land, Hatfield, Hadley, Pelham, Cold Spring (now Belcher-
town), and Springfield.   All of these churches were represented at the anniversary celebration except Pelham and
Enfield, and the omission of Enfield was due to an over-
sight on the part of the Memorial Committee, who did not
discover till too late that what was Enfield, Hampshire
County, Mass., in Edwards' time was not the town of that
name now in the county, but Enfield, Conn.

come and introduced the speakers. The
Chairman of the Memorial Committee made
his report and presented the tablet, which
was then unveiled by Mr. Charles Atwood
Edwards, of New York, the oldest living de-
scendant of the theologian in the line of
Jonathan Edwards the younger. Immediately following this ceremony, the chorus
choir of the church, under the leadership of
the choirmaster, Mr. Ralph L. Baldwin, rendered an anthem, composed for the occasion
by Dr. Benjamin C. Blodgett, of Smith College, on the words of St. Paul, Rom. xi. 33–
36 : " O the depth of the riches both of the
wisdom and knowledge of God ! how un-
searchable are his judgments, and his ways
past finding out ! For who hath known the
mind of the Lord ? or who hath been his
counsellor ? Or who hath first given to him,
and it shall be recompensed unto him again ?
For of him, and through him, and to him,
are all things : to whom be glory for ever.
Amen." No words of Scripture, it has well
been said, correspond closer to Edwards' sublime conceptions. The principal addresses
were made by the Rev. Professor Alexander
V. G. Allen, D. D., of Cambridge, on the

Place of Edwards in History; by the Rev.
Professor Egbert C. Smyth, D. D., of Andover, on the Influence of Edwards on the
Spiritual Life of New England; and by the
Rev. George A. Gordon, D. D., of Boston, on
the Significance of Edwards To-Day. The
well-known hymn by Edwards' grandson,
Timothy Dwight, "I love thy kingdom,
Lord," and the hymn, "For all thy saints,"
were sung by the congregation. The vener-
able Timothy Dwight, former president of
Yale University, and fourth in descent from
the Timothy Dwight, of Northampton, who
married Edwards' daughter, Mary, in the
year of the dismissal, pronounced the bene-
diction. On the following Sunday morning,
the Rev. Dr. Rose delivered an historical address on Edwards in Northampton.

The above addresses, which are here given
to a wider public, are not mere eulogies;
they are a serious attempt on the part of
sympathetic, but by no means uncritical students to form a just estimate of a great man
in some of his most fundamental relations,
to determine his place in history, to appreciate his character and influence, and to discover in him, amid whatever was temporary

and accidental, elements of essential value, a present and permanent significance. In the short time allowed to the several speakers, it was impossible, of course, to treat, even cursorily, of all the aspects of his genius. There was no attempt, for instance, to set forth his importance as a philosopher. An address by the editor on the Early Idealism of Edwards, suggested by the occasion and delivered before students of philosophy at Wellesley and Smith colleges, is here inserted by request; but it only partially supplies the omission by presenting the evidence of Edwards' originality and by indicating the bearing of his conception on the general interpretation of his thought and personality. There is greatly needed from a competent writer a thorough study of his philosophy as a whole. A still more serious omission in the view of many will seem the failure to attempt any accurate estimate of his value and influence as a theologian. This, however, is a large task and requires a more delicate handling than is now the fashion, when Edwards is supposed to represent the final divorce of theology from life, and to be sufficiently refuted by a reference to Holmes' brilliant

satire of a One-Hoss Shay. Still the fact
that on an historic occasion, after the lapse of
a century and a half, some of his most appre-
ciative students and ardent admirers chose to
represent him less as a theologian than as a
prophet of the Christian faith, an interpreter
of human life, a force in religious experience,
and profess to see in him less affinity with
Calvin than with Dante, is sufficiently significant. Significant, too, is the very out-
spoken criticism of some points in his theology by perhaps the leading representative at
the present time of the Puritan tradition in
New England. But though these addresses
make no claim, either singly or collectively,
to be exhaustive, they will be found, it is
hoped, to set forth their subject, as far as
they do treat it, in a fresh and suggestive
manner, to help somewhat to bring out in
true historical perspective the real Edwards,
to remove something from the popular mis-
conceptions of him, and to show the essential quality of his greatness. They are published, therefore, not merely as a memorial of
an interesting event in the history of a local
church, but as a contribution to the understanding of an event of wider historical sig-

nificance, and of a great but only too often misjudged character.

The representation of the Memorial Tablet in the Appendix is from a photograph of the unfinished clay model without the frame. It cannot be considered satisfactory, but the tablet in place is difficult to photograph, and in fact no photograph of it suitable for reproduction has yet been made. The portraits of Mr. and Mrs. Edwards are reproductions of the original paintings of 1740 from photographs by Giles Bishop and Son, of New London, Conn. These paintings, recently in the possession of the late Mr. Eugene Edwards, of Stonington, Conn., are the originals of which all the portraits of Jonathan Edwards and of Mrs. Edwards are directly or indirectly copies. The portrait of the theologian in the present volume may fairly claim to be the most authentic likeness of him yet published. The accompanying portrait of Mrs. Edwards, new probably to most readers, will surely be of welcome interest to all who justly appreciate her influence on him.

The editor takes this opportunity to express his thanks to the writers of the several papers for their coöperation, and to the editors of the Congregationalist and the Philosophical Review, respectively, for permission to reprint Dr. Gordon's article and his own.

THE PLACE OF EDWARDS IN HISTORY

BY PROFESSOR A. V. G. ALLEN, D. D.

JONATHAN EDWARDS

THE PLACE OF EDWARDS IN HISTORY

IT is one of the opportunities of the present age that we may recognize the essential motive in a great man apart from beliefs with which his name has been associated. When a man has become truly great he passes over into the possession of humanity, and is no longer the peculiar property of any sect or school of opinion. The memory of Jonathan Edwards not only haunts the New England churches, but is cherished by those whose larger interest is the common welfare of Christendom. There was something in Edwards, something that he did or was in himself, which has survived the lapse of time, so that after a hundred and fifty years have passed it has been possible to raise a monument to him in the church which he served, and to call together his fellow townsmen in an effort to do him honor. In some way Edwards has reflected honor upon the human race, which entitles him to the epithet of greatness. That epithet cannot be retained if given where it is not deserved, and when it is deserved it cannot be withheld. In a certain sense, the highest sense, Edwards was right when he held that the number of the elect was few. And among those few he takes his place, — elect and chosen souls, whom God *foreknows* and therefore *calls*.

It is a source of regret and complaint with some that more is not told of the man himself. We would fain know his personal characteristics, what kind of a man he was in the daily intercourse of life, — those simple, human touches which bring a man vividly before our imagination. But of such information about Edwards little has been preserved. His personality was absorbed in his thought. He was carried out of himself and forgot himself in the pursuit of ideas and eternal truths. He identified himself with an ideal aim, and by that he is known. It is in vain that we seek to live with him as with ordinary men. Had we associated with him when he tabernacled in the flesh, we should have hardly known more of him than we do to-day. He is invested with a certain air of vagueness and of mystery, which it is not likely will ever be dispelled.

But there is one personal characteristic in the life of Edwards, so real, so beautiful, that with it we might almost be content, had nothing else been told ; which in itself reveals to us the man so essentially, that we hardly need to search further in our effort to delineate him. Although it is a familiar picture, we never tire of looking at it, as painted for us in his own exquisite words. The visitor to the town of Northampton gains a new sense of the reality and intensity of Edwards' experience, when recalling that he came here in 1727, at the age of twenty-three, bringing with him his wife, who had attained the age of seventeen. I will not apologize, then, for repeating the familiar description which Edwards wrote of Sarah Pierrepont when she was a young girl of thirteen : —

They say that there is a young lady in New Haven who is beloved of that great Being who made and rules the world, and there are certain seasons in which this great Being, in some way or other invisible, comes to her and fills her mind with exceeding sweet delight, and that she hardly cares for anything except to meditate on Him; that she expects after a while to be raised up out of the world and caught up into heaven; being assured that He loves her too well to let her remain at a distance from Him always. There she is to dwell with Him and to be ravished with His love and delight forever. Therefore, if you present all the world before her, with the richest of its treasures, she cares not for it, and is unmindful of any pain or affliction. She has a strange sweetness in her mind and singular purity in her affections; is most just and conscientious in all her conduct; and you could not persuade her to do anything wrong or sinful if you would give her all the world, lest she should offend this great Being. She is of a wonderful calmness and universal benevolence of mind; especially after this great God has manifested Himself to her mind. She will sometimes go about from place to place singing sweetly; and seems to be always full of joy and pleasure, and no one knows for what. She loves to be alone, walking in the fields and groves, and seems to have some one invisible always conversing with her.

This event in the life of Edwards may have been the beginning of his conversion; this the way by which he was led to the knowledge and love of God. Any adequate comment upon the passage is impossible. We must leave it as it stands, one of the most exquisite things in literature, — the revelation of a beautiful soul. But there is one utterance which may be put in comparison, — only one other, — and that is from Dante, when he first saw Beatrice, who was then also a young girl, like Sarah Pierrepont, and in her ninth year : —

Her dress on that day was a most noble colour, a subdued and goodly crimson, girdled and adorned in such sort as best suited with her very tender age. At that moment, I say most truly, that the spirit of life, which hath its dwelling in the secretest chamber of the heart, began to tremble so violently that the least pulses of my body shook therewith, and in trembling it said these words, "Behold the deity, which is stronger than I, who coming to me will rule within me."

One inference which we are entitled to draw from these two passages is the affinity, the spiritual affinity, between the men who wrote them. Edwards has often been compared with Calvin and with Augustine, and, so far as his theological opinions are concerned, the comparison is correct. He maintained substantially the Calvinistic theology, as it had first been formulated by St. Augustine. The work which he did, and the age in which he lived, resembled those of his great predecessors. But he also did another

work more distinctly his own. We can
hardly imagine St. Augustine, or John Calvin, or the Scottish reformer, John Knox, or
Baxter, or Owen, writing about woman such
words as Edwards wrote of Sarah Pierrepont,
or Dante wrote of Beatrice.

There is, then, no casual accidental resemblance here. The deepest affinity of Edwards
was not that with Calvin or with Augustine,
but with the great Florentine poet. Upon
that comparison I wish for a few moments
to dwell. If I am right we shall see Edwards in a different but also a truer light
than that, in which according to the popular
tradition he has been presented.

How shall we define the quality common
alike to the poet Dante and the theologian
Jonathan Edwards? It must be that both
had the tendency to idealize the world, to
transfigure as in a vision the life of man,
carrying it to the furthest possible extreme,
reading the divine through the human, till
they almost deified the human, through its
capacity for the divine. As we study the
ages in which they lived, the comparison
grows clearer. Dante was the precursor of
the movement, known as the Renaissance,

in the fourteenth and fifteenth centuries, which brought back again to the world the simple, human outlook of the ages before Augustine arose. In other words, he was a poet and prepared the way for an outburst of poetry after the long, hard, sterile ages, lasting for more than a thousand years, in which no voice of poetry was heard. The great movement which Dante inaugurated had in it seeds of evil and of moral corruption, as well as of truth and beauty and goodness. Against the license which followed in its wake Calvin and Ignatius Loyola both protested with such force that the movement seemed to come to an end, and its higher work to have been almost undone. Humanism lost its prestige in the latter half of the sixteenth century, with one momentous exception, which was Shakespeare.

Jonathan Edwards stood like Dante at the beginning of a new age and at the dividing of the waters, after the long régime of Puritanism in the English-speaking world. He too was the precursor of a great humanitarian movement which went on accumulating in power till it became the controlling force in the nineteenth century, manifesting itself

in literature, in art, in science and political
economy, till it culminated in the sociological
movements of the age in which we live.   As
Dante sought to bind the old and new together, giving his sanction to the age that
was going out, and, as a profound student of
Aquinas, consecrating with the poetic imagination the Catholic régime of the Middle
Ages, its worship and its theology, so Edwards sought to bind the spirit which was beginning to be felt in his age with the Puritan
theology as he had received it by tradition
from his ancestors, and intermingled, as it
were, with his blood.   Dante and Edwards
may both alike be studied from opposite
points of view, and from the point of view
which we take will appear to be different
men, with divergent if not contradictory
aims.   But it is perfectly legitimate to regard Edwards as the precursor of the humanitarian movement, as it is to regard
Dante as the precursor of the Renaissance.
It is evident at a glance the line of descent,
— the pupil and disciple of Edwards was
Hopkins of Newport, who first led in America the movement for the abolition of human
slavery.   And as Hopkins was the pupil of

Edwards, so did Dr. Channing declare himself the pupil of Hopkins, from whose doctrine of disinterested benevolence he drew the inspiration for modern humanitarianism, of which he became the prophet and the exponent.

Dante and Edwards were alike in this, that they possessed the intellectual, poetic imagination. Both applied their gifts to the involution of the kingdom of God, turning it inside out, that its inmost contents might be seen and known. What others had done for the kingdom of this world, or the study of political motives, they did for the church and religion. Dante had the advantage of living in the world's centre, and at one of the great moments of history. Edwards lived in what was then an obscure corner, the remote edge of civilization, and in a dull, uninteresting age, which gave no promise of a future. But their work was substantially the same. It shows the transcendent genius of Edwards that he rose above his limitations, and has given such a picture of the reality and rich variety of the interior life of religion as was never given before.

That was Edwards' most distinctive work.

His characteristic writings, which are also the most valuable, are not after all the treatises on the Freedom of the Will or on Original Sin. These may have been disproved. Carrying a system by dialectic, as Edwards did to its logical conclusion, was to make it consistent indeed, but also to doom it to sterility. His best books are these: the Sermon on Spiritual Light, the Narrative of Surprising Conversions, the Distinguishing Marks of a Work of Grace, Thoughts on the Revival, and finally, his greatest work, on the Religious Affections. These correspond in their way to the Divine Comedy: they are kindred in spirit and purpose. If Dante went through hell and purgatory and heaven to get their secret inner life and make manifest their hidden principles, so Edwards studied with intense devotion the inmost nature of the soul in its relationship with God and under the action of the divine Grace.

Guarding against the tendency to carry these comparisons too far, let us note another resemblance between Dante and Edwards: both were driven into banishment and exile, and for no fault of their own. Each of them experienced the tragedy of life brought around by circumstances which it was impossible to overcome, — what seems like the working of a blind and cruel fate.

To this comparison may be added another. As Dante was conducted through the heavens by Beatrice, so was Edwards guided in his spiritual quest by the influence of his wife. It was an ideal marriage with Sarah Pierrepont. Any one who has studied the life and writings of Edwards will see that in the bewilderment of that mighty upheaval of the New England churches, known as the Great Awakening, Edwards greatly depended on her character and testimony. He could never for his own part succeed in gaining those rapt experiences in the soul of which others boasted. He was an onlooker, a believer in them, and yet at times he may have doubted their reality. What made him sure that the work of grace in Northampton and elsewhere was no illusion, that the great Jehovah had actually come down into New England to move the hearts of the people, was the testimony and the character of his wife. For it was an awful moment which followed the great revival, till it seemed as though religion, faith, hope, and charity were like to perish from the land. Edwards, according to his own statement, made the character of his wife and her experience the standard both for judgment of errors and for confirmation of the truth. Thus after describing the inner moods of the working of the divine Grace, as she had known them, and giving to the world her religious confessions, he exclaims that this could have been no other than the peace of God which passeth all understanding, — the joy and peace in believing which is unspeakable and full of glory. " If such things are enthusiasm and the fruits of a distempered brain, let my brain be evermore possessed of that happy distemper. If this be distraction, I pray God that the world of mankind may all be seized with this benign, meek, beneficial, beautiful, glorious distraction."

And once more I am tempted to seek in Dante the fittest word to be put in comparison with this outburst of Edwards' sure and loving confidence. In the Vita Nuova, Dante speaks of Beatrice after her death : —

It was given unto me to behold a very wonderful vision : wherein I saw things which determined me that I would say nothing further of this most blessed one, until such time as I could discourse more worthily concerning her. And to this end I labor all I can as she well knoweth. Wherefore if it be His pleasure through whom is the life of all things, that my life continue with me for a few years, it is my hope that I shall yet write concerning her what hath not before been written of any woman. After which, may it seem good unto Him who is the Master of grace, that my spirit should go hence to behold the glory of my lady, that blessed Beatrice, who now gazeth continually on His face who is blessed through all the ages.

As Edwards lay on his deathbed at Princeton it was noticed that he said but little. There were none of the raptures of David Brainerd to be recorded; he made no allusion to his books, to the labors of his life, or to the fortunes of the church of God; but he spoke to his daughter, and the words are recorded : —

Give my kindest love to my dear wife, and tell her that the *uncommon* union which has so long subsisted between us has been of such a nature as I trust is spiritual, and therefore will continue forever.

My object in dealing with this phase of the life of Edwards is to show that in constitution and temperament he was a different man from Augustine or from Calvin, that he is not, paradoxical as it may seem to say it, —

he is not really so great as a theologian as
he is when viewed as a poetic interpreter of
life.   He never wrote, so far as we know, a
line of poetry.   But he had the poet's imagination, and tenderness, and insight combined with an unsurpassed gift for spiritual
speculation.   That combination is one of the
rarest gifts which God ever makes to men.

I wish that I had time to illustrate from
his writings the poetic element which pervades the prose of Jonathan Edwards.
When he drops his dialectic and becomes
unconscious of his power, when the simple
nature of the man is left free to speak, there
is something so exquisite and so beautiful in
thought and language that we feel he is
entitled to a place among the masters of
speech.   The farewell sermon of John Henry
Newman, as he was leaving the Church of
England, is often referred to as one of the
highest specimens of English prose, but as
we study Edwards it almost seems as if Newman might have taken him for his teacher,
and caught from him the secret of his skill.

And now I am led to ask the 'question,
why it is that Edwards has been so misrepre-
sented as to have been a name of horror and

execration with many ; that he should be remembered chiefly for a babe-damning mon-
ster; that the sermon preached at Enfield
should be more often quoted than any of his
other writings ; that because of that utterance
his other work should suffer and be held of
no account. Those who go to his books
turn to the imprecatory sermons and there
they stop, wondering at the man who could
have found it in him to say such things.
One answer to the question must surely be
that the tragedy of human life encompassed
him as it also encompassed Dante. Evil had
been done, and he has been held responsible
because of his greatness. Yet the truth is
that those terrific sermons where he pictures
the sufferings of the damned in hell are the
least original of all the writings of Edwards.
There is less of Edwards in them. He was
hard, to be sure ; inhuman it seems to the
last degree, but so also was Dante, as he
leaves Virgil in hell, after his work as a
guide is over, with no compunction for his
fate. Dante could look on unmoved at the
prospect of the whole heathen world in endless suffering, and so did Edwards. Edwards
differs from Dante in that he takes no inter-

est in the Inferno which he draws. He is inferior also to the great Florentine in this respect, that he made no effort to adjust the penalty to the offense. He does not recognize, as Dante did, how the penalty must grow out of the nature of the sin. With Edwards it is all arbitrary and mechanical, without difference and distinction. He did not give his mind to the subject, or he would not have used perpetually the same crude figures and illustrations which had been so often used before him. He would have invented a new imagery and employed his speculative capacity in new requirements of torture. Instead of that he talks the same dialect that Tertullian used, or preachers of the Middle Ages, when they described the tortures of the lost. The Inferno of Edwards is lacking in originality; it is crude and commonplace in its descriptions, and even vulgar. But everything is intense, and that was Edwards' misfortune and the result of his poetic temperament. Whatever he did had a touch of his genius; he could not be like common men. It was the fashion of the time to scare men into religion by these methods, as in Dante's age it was the tradition that the heathen world was in hell. In this respect Edwards only followed his age. Shall we condemn him that he did not rise above it, or that when he did preach on these subjects he surpassed others in the intensity of his utterance, as he surpassed them in the majesty of all his powers ?

Edwards, as I have said, was not greatly interested in the fearful picture which he drew. The evidence of this statement must lie in comparing what he has written on hell with his other writings. He was at his best and greatest, most original and creative, when he describes the *divine love*, or when he attempts to draw the glories of the life of heaven. Then his speculative genius was set free, and on the wings of the spiritual imagination he soared into regions where it is difficult to follow, without his own spiritual endowment. I do not know of anything in the literature of heaven which surpasses what Edwards has written. There is no trace of his having read the Paradiso, but he did not need to read it for any necessity he had to gain stimulus or material of thought. That fascinating combination of the poetic imagination with religious faith and speculative

capacity may here be seen in its richest mani-
festation. To the man that could write of
heaven as Edwards did, it must seem as
though compliance with, or inability to rise
above, the prevailing homiletic methods might
be forgiven. Still, it cannot be forgotten.
It forms an essential part of a tragedy which
was enacting, and from which Edwards could
not escape.

And thus we are naturally led to touch
briefly upon that event in the life of Edwards, his banishment from Northampton,
whose one hundred and fiftieth anniversary
we are observing. Edwards, I think, was
lacking in the sense of humor, so indispen-
sable to the right appreciation of human affairs. There is one passage in his writings
which may or may not have been humor-
ously intended, but which now carries such a
reminder. He is speaking of the devil, and
he is led to ask why it is, when God will
suffer nothing to be accomplished which is
not for his own glory, the devil, with his accumulated experience of failures, should still
persist in his deep-laid contrivances, which
must always end in his discomfiture. To
this question says Edwards, " I answer, that,

although the devil be exceeding crafty and subtle, yet he is one of the greatest fools and blockheads in the world." When Edwards wrote this passage there is no means of determining; but it could hardly have been after the defeat and mortification which ended in his exile from Northampton. For that event is so strangely confused, that one is tempted to feel as if neither God nor man could be held responsible ; that it was rather the working of an evil genius who, if he could accomplish no other end, could yet make trouble and bring dire calamity.

I do not understand by this present occasion, with its impressive ceremony of unveiling a monument to Jonathan Edwards, that the congregation of the First Church in Northampton is thereby seeking to make amends for the past, or any act of repentance for evil and injustice done by its ancestors. Edwards was right in his attitude, and yet the church was not in the wrong. There are two sides to the question. At the distance of one hundred and fifty years we should be guilty of a greater wrong, if we had not improved the opportunity which time has brought to see the issue in a larger light.

If Edwards were living to-day we must believe he at least would have unraveled the complex situation which in his lifetime he failed to understand ; that if he were now delivering his memorable Farewell Sermon he would have somewhat to add ; and he himself would admit that, in the Providence of God, things had come to such a pass, there was no alternative but his rejection from the church and the town which he loved.

The cause of the rejection of Edwards was not merely the opposition of a prominent family in the parish, nor was it merely an unfortunate case of discipline which had alienated his parishioners, nor was it only that in his preaching he had lost his hold upon the congregation. These things contributed to the tragedy, and may explain some of the unfortunate methods adopted to get rid of a pastor who had become obnoxious ; while the deeper cause for the suspicion, the alienation, the hostility, lies far beneath and remote from these secondary circumstances.

When Edwards was writing his treatise on the Religious Affections, the last book which he wrote before leaving Northampton,

MRS. EDWARDS

and the greatest of all his works, he was not thinking as he portrayed the character of a Christian man, in such exalted, sublimated ways, as to make it an almost superhuman attainment, — as he painted with an exquisite touch the refinements of Christian love and purity, and singleness of heart, he was not thinking of the reverse side of the picture, or urging the inference that those who had not the religious affections towards God, which he was describing in such beautiful but transcendent ways, must be banished forever from God's presence. As I have said before, his Inferno was not an original, creative picture wherein he delighted, or had studied to elaborate as Milton or Dante had done. For the moment it was in the background, as he gave his spirit wings to rise to the contemplation of celestial love.

But it was in the foreground of the consciousness of the church in Northampton, and in the consciousness also of the New England people. The imprecatory sermons not only of Edwards but of many others had overdone the appeal to fear in the Great Awakening, and had accomplished their

work too well. When Edwards now pro-
ceeded to draw his ideal sketch of what a con-
verted man must be, as in his book on the
Religious Affections, he was unconsciously
straining the situation till it became impossible and a catastrophe was well-nigh inevitable.
If at this point he had stopped, it might have
been averted. Edwards, however, now proposed a practical step, an innovation in the
organization of the church, by which only
those who made a confession of faith should
be admitted to the Lord's Supper. So long
as he was content to hold up the impossible
ideal standard, and to leave the table of the
Lord free and open, with the conscience of
the worshiper as its safeguard, there would
have been no friction. When he proposed
a test of admission to the Lord's Supper,
setting aside the usage of his grandfather,
the catastrophe followed immediately. It
was in words a very moderate test, asking
only for the conscious purpose of love to
God and a desire to serve Him, but Edwards
had for more than twenty years been seeking
to show how much the love of man toward
God must mean and what His service de-
manded, together with the fearful alternative

of what their absence must mean. And so, unwittingly, and by his very greatness, he seemed to be making a church and religion impossible. It was for these things that the church in Northampton was contending when they insisted that he must go. The people could not come up to his standard. No man living could feel sure that he was a Christian or that he loved God, when judging himself by Edwards' standard. The church in Northampton was seeking to save religion and the worship of God and the fellowship of the church from the utter wreck which to their horrified imaginations appeared so near, so imminent. They had in mind their children also, and their highest interests, for the alternative was fearful. It was indeed an awful moment in the history of religion in New England, — the conflict between the ideal, drawn by a master hand, as it had never been drawn before, and the lower reality which was practical and possible. This disruption of the relationship between pastor and people was a harbinger of greater evils yet to come. Years afterward the church in Northampton fell into line with the other churches adopting a test for

admission to the communion; yet, it could
not with dignity or safety have done so
under the ministry of Jonathan Edwards.
The banishment of Edwards was indeed the
salvation of the church in Northampton.
And what a tragedy it was! What lessons
it contains for men in every age! Although
it happened in a remote time and concerned
at first only one congregation, yet it is of
world-wide interest and reflects in miniature
a world process. In a lesser sphere and
within narrower limits what was happening
in New England was the same in principle
with what took place in the later Middle
Ages, when the abstraction of the papacy
was pushed to its remotest consequences;
when those who aimed at the best and the
highest overshot the mark; when scholastic
theologians by their dialectic reduced the
mediæval theory to absolute consistency,
carrying theories, indeed, to their logical
result, but blocking the way of true religion
and making the church impossible. The experience of life is something greater than
theological consistency, and to this final test
all theories must come.

    And oh, the depth of the pathos revealed

in the sufferings of Edwards. Even at this distance of time we sigh, as we think of so great a man, the greatest of his age in the kingdom of God, at home or abroad, humiliated, mortified, disgraced, carrying with him to his grave a mortal wound. The pathos of his life is apparent henceforth in all his work, first in his Farewell Sermon, then in that voluminous book he wrote in self-defense, called the Humble Inquiry or sometimes a Reply to Williams, which was the more valuable to him because it served his purpose as a vent for his moral indignation, — a work almost unreadable now, yet even to one who attempts it, revealing that there were two sides to the question. When that work had been disposed of he next summoned all the powers which God had given him, to what he believed to be a greater task. He thought that he saw beneath the question of the terms of admission to the Lord's Supper a deeper issue in the catastrophe of his life. What had caused his discomfiture, and to his mind was at the root of all the evil which afflicted the church, was the growing tendency to abandon the traditional theology of the Puritan Fathers.

He had thought so when he began his ministry, and now that the leisure had come, in his retirement at Stockbridge, he devoted his unwearied genius to the defense of those theological tenets, which the age was calling in question. In quick succession his books followed each other, — treatises on Original Sin; the Nature of True Virtue; the Last End of God in the Creation; and the most famous work of all, the Freedom of the Will.

Through all these books runs one common purpose, to bring back again the world to God. The danger, the evil he deprecated was this, that men would think God had left the world to take care of itself, or that without God's aid they could accomplish their salvation. He had indeed grounds for fear, for such was the prevailing mood of the first half of the eighteenth century in England and France, Germany and America. God, as Edwards believed, could not govern the world if men were free, — therefore he labored to prove that the freedom of the will in the ordinary sense was impossible. Then he turned to demonstrate the doctrine of original sin, by which man had lost his

freedom, and became utterly depraved, help-
less, and ruined. Thence it followed that
only those whom God elected to save could
be saved. These were but few; the rest
were left to suffer the endless consequences
of the divine wrath. Such in outline was
the theology which Edwards defended.

To these two books, on the Freedom of
the Will and on Original Sin, one common
remark applies. They are apparently philosophical treatises, or it may be theological,
whichever we may please to call them, but
they glow with a burning intensity of fervor,
and there is a passionate vehemence so unusual in purely dogmatic treatises as to indicate some extraordinary motive in their composition. The treatise on the Freedom of
the Will is no dispassionate discussion in the
dry light of the intellect; it could not be,
when, as we are told, it was written in the
short space of three months. Edwards was
still suffering from the agony of his separation from Northampton. He had intimated
in his Farewell Sermon that the deadly influences of Arminianism had crept into the town
despite his watchfulness. It was to Arminianism in the last resort that his banishment

was owing. His book on the Freedom of
the Will constitutes his apologia. The personality of Edwards is there, giving to the
argument something of additional vitality
and human charm. The personality of the
great author, as in the Divine Comedy, in-
fuses its reasoning, till it stands as a monument to the bitter experiences of a human
soul.

In Edwards' books on the Nature of True
Virtue, and on the Last End of God, in
the treatise on Grace also, and in the treatise on the Trinity, which it is hoped may
yet see the light, there is a tone which shows
he had not yet completed the circle of his
thought. He saw things in remote vistas toward which he was still traveling, when death
overtook him. All that it was in him to say
to the world had not been said. His mind
was so vast in its range, and his power of the
abstract reason, that it seems as if he could
have done anything within the compass of
mortal powers. It is possible, too, had his
life been spared, that he would have found
rest and repose in the contemplation of nature, for whose investigation he had shown
such astounding capacity when a boy. To

ground the relationship between God and man in the order of the natural creation would have given the relief from that spiritual tension which had been the defect of his spiritual philosophy, and had led to his own defeat.

There are three stages in the life of our human sonship to God. In the first place we are God's own children by creation, and as such are the objects of his love. In the second place we are his children by the redemption of Christ, who, as the Eternal Son dwelling in the flesh, has claimed all men for his brethren. And, thirdly, we are God's children in the last and highest sense, by the sanctification of the Holy Spirit. It was only upon the last of these that Edwards cared to dwell. But, here, his work was great and imperishable. If any one would know the mysterious life of the human soul in communion with the infinite spirit of God, he will find it drawn by Edwards with a loving, painstaking care such as is not elsewhere to be found in religious literature.

THE INFLUENCE OF EDWARDS ON THE SPIRITUAL LIFE OF NEW ENGLAND

BY PROFESSOR EGBERT C. SMYTH, D. D.

THE INFLUENCE OF EDWARDS ON THE SPIRITUAL LIFE OF NEW ENGLAND

WITHIN the time assigned me you will not expect even a rapid sketch of the religious history of New England. What has Edwards been to us these hundred and fifty years? What, in that which has been truest, greatest in New England, its strong, deep, continuous spiritual life? This I understand to be the essence of the subject I am invited to present. It brings to the front Edwards' transcendent spiritual personality. It says: See him, and you gain the clearest insight into what he has wrought.

Yet when your purpose is thus interpreted, my task, though somewhat simplified, seems, if possible, even more arduous. He is so great, so beautiful, so high! I can but think of Dante's words, as, in the empyrean, he turns with his eyes to Beatrice, "If," he writes, "what has been said of her so far as here were all included in a single praise, it

would be little to furnish out this turn. The
beauty which I saw transcends measure not
only by us, but truly I believe that its Maker
alone can enjoy it all." [1]

Happily you have given me a favoring
sign. In the tablet now unveiled Edwards
stands forth as a Prophet of the Lord, a
Witness, a Seer; and his life and influence
are interpreted from the Book on whose
words he meditated day and night: " The
law of truth was in his mouth, and unrighteousness was not found in his lips: he walked
with Me in peace and uprightness, and did
turn many away from iniquity."

I desire to speak of him as such a Witness.

I. *As a Witness to the spiritual life in
man and to its Divine origin and attesta-
tion.*

What interests us most in him is the singular purity and clearness with which, through
his life, this spiritual element appears. Its
effect is heightened by the range and variety
of his powers, their keenness and tirelessness.
It is not a mere factor in a great career, a

[1] *Paradiso*, xxx. 16–21, Norton's translation.

strain in a noble character, an effusion of
sensibility, a play of fancy, a higher flight of
a lofty imagination.   It is his calmest mood,
as well as his most impassioned warning or
pleading, his profoundest reasoning, his clearest insight, his widest outlook.   It is the
solid earth on which he treads, its sleeping
rocks and firm set hills, the skies into whose
depths he gazes, the incense of the little
flower in spring tide, the praises of heaven.
We feel it wherever we come in contact with
him, — on the banks of the Hudson, in the
fields at Saybrook, in " the woods and solitary places " he frequented for " meditation,
soliloquy, and prayer, and converse with God,"
singing forth at such times his contempla-
tions, in his joy as he ' views the clouds and
sees the lightnings play and hears the majestic and awful voice of God's thunder.'   It is
the boy building with some schoolmates
their rustic oratory, the idealist at New
Haven independent of Berkeley, the preacher,
the man.   We meet it in all that he does or
says or writes, from his earliest known composition, refuting with playful irony the no-
tion that the soul is material, to his tender
farewell message to his wife assuring her of

his trust 'that the uncommon union which
had so long subsisted between them had been
of such a nature as is spiritual, and therefore
would continue forever.'

I would emphasize this spirituality as a
fact, — a supreme, a momentous one to him
who has eyes to see. Here is a man, bone
of our bone, born among us, living always,
save for a few months, near the river that
courses through the length of New England,
a man not lacking in any quality of homely
wisdom, not without much of the shrewdness,
even, of our people, retiring and fond of soli-
tude, yet, from his young manhood, conspic-
uous to keen-eyed men, and of sincerity
unimpeachable, who not only knew God, but
knew that he knew Him, not perfectly,
far from it, but personally and surely,
and who puts this estimate on such knowledge: "He that sees the beauty of holiness,
or true moral good, sees the greatest and
most important thing in the world, which is
the fulness of all things, without which all
the world is empty, yea, worse than nothing.
Unless this is seen, nothing is seen that is
worth the seeing; for there is no other true
excellency or beauty. Unless this be under-

stood, nothing is understood worthy the exercise of the noble faculty of understanding. This is the beauty of the Godhead, the divinity of divinity (if I may so speak), the good of the infinite fountain of good. Without this, God himself (if that were possible) would be an infinite evil, we ourselves had better never have been ; and there had better have been no being. He therefore in effect knows nothing that knows not this ; his knowledge is but the shadow of knowledge, or the *form of knowledge*, as the apostle calls it. . . . And well may regeneration, in which this divine sense is given to the soul by its Creator, be represented as opening the blind eyes, raising the dead, and bringing a person into a new world." [1]

Edwards was unflagging and relentless in his endeavors to discriminate between a false or illusory and a genuine, spiritual experience. His treatise concerning Religious Affections carries self-inspection and scrutiny to an extreme, and needs balancing by an equally effective presentation of the objects of faith, and of their operation through

[1] " Religious Affections," pt. iii. § 4 (*Works*, v. 158, Dwight's ed.).

organic constitutions and forms, and by laws
of spiritual nurture and growth. But this
excess of subjective analysis has in this particular one advantage. It leaves more distinct, impressive, commanding, the testimony
of a Seer to the source and reality of the
spiritual life itself. He is a witness unsurpassed in his intellectual and critical power,
no dreamer, no rhapsodist, no " God-intoxi-
cated man," no mystic even, if by this is
meant one who loses himself in his ecstasies,
an atmosphere, or breath of an atmosphere,
without a world, a flux or efflux without a
source or principle or law. Edwards *sees*,
not dreams. He saw himself and men, as
well as God. When one says to me : " God
cannot be known," I reply, " Edwards knew
Him ; " or " Matter and Force are all," I answer, " Edwards was more than they." Test
your knowledge or your doubt of it, as he
did both his blindness and his vision. Test,
as rigorously as he, as unsparingly, from top
to bottom, through and through, and drive
your fallacies as far as he, that is, out of the
world and into the abysses of Folly and
Night. A world is not wholly dark in which
Jesus has said, *I am the Light*, and in

which other lights kindled at that Source
have shone resplendent, even though it be
that we see here but the breaking of the
day.

Edwards walked these streets. You have
written on your tablet, " He walked with
God." We may not simply take his word.
If you and I would know God, we too must
each find Him, or rather be found of Him.
But Edwards has gone over the road and
seen the vision. There is no lion in the
path he followed and illumined, waiting to
devour the wayfarer to that home of the
soul, that peace of God, which he first knew
for himself, then drew to it others with him.

Nor of less value has been his influence
in this respect on our theology, both homiletic and theoretic. For a hundred years
and more, and especially from Edwards' day,
this has had a strongly marked intellectual
and ethical character, and this, unbalanced
by influences from long-established and familiar forms of ecclesiastical authority, or
constant liturgical presentations of the objects of faith, sacred events in the life of our
Lord, or the experiences of sainted men and
women. Rationalism and Moralism always

are attendant upon such a situation. Yet
there has been far less of either of these than
might have been anticipated, mainly perhaps
from the generally Biblical character of the
preaching, and as included in this, from the
emphasis laid upon spiritual regeneration,
and the Christian life and society as a fellowship of men with Christ and with God.
How great in all this has been the influence
of Edwards I need but suggest.

II. What has been said seems to me to
touch upon what must be deemed of chief
importance in any proper estimate of Edwards' religious influence. It needs, however,
to be accompanied by another presentation,
namely, one that recognizes *the directness
and fearlessness of his appeal, in promot-
ing religion, to reason.* Though this power
of the soul is not in his view the proper cause
of religion, since faith arises from the immediate operation in the human spirit of the
Divine, yet faith implies reason and is reasonable. One may easily be misled on this
point by the tremendous stress he lays on
the necessity of grace. But it is noteworthy
how constantly he appeals to reason, and
this even when he is enforcing, in the most

earnest and decisive way, the creative power and prerogative of the Holy Spirit. Look, for instance, at his method in his famous sermon on the Reality of Spiritual Light, a light " immediately imparted to the soul by God, of a different nature from any that is obtained by natural means." His argument is, first, the doctrine is scriptural; second, it is rational. " Christ's peace," he says elsewhere, " is a *reasonable* peace and rest of soul." [1]

In Edwards' time the psychological terminology with which we are more or less familiar was undeveloped. He is so careful a reasoner that I sometimes think we are more embarrassed in understanding him by our own nomenclature than by his. In the sermon, for instance, on Spiritual Light, he is careful to say that " if we take *reason* strictly, — not for the faculty of mental perception in general, but for ratiocination or a power of inferring by arguments, — the perceiving of spiritual beauty and excellency no more belongs to reason than it belongs to the sense of feeling to perceive colors." [2] He thus recognizes that there is a larger, though

[1] *Works*, vi. 133.   [2] *Ibid.* vi. 186.

less precise, meaning of the word reason.
The soul he believed to be an immediate
creation of God, and reason inheres in it.
This word reason, we are learning to recognize more definitely perhaps than did he,
covers properly many and varied mental operations, — those which are most purely intellectual, like mathematical calculations, those
also which are ethical, — moral intuitions
and judgments, and those as well which are
distinctively spiritual and yet include both
what is ethical and intellectual.[1] In this
supreme sense of spiritual intelligence reason is, in the highest degree, involved in
Edwards' apprehension of spiritual religion.
His sense of the sweetness, beauty, majesty,
glory of God, his delight in the harmony of
his perfections and the expressions of his
love, imply spiritual perceptions in which
reason in all its grades and forms and func-
tions is involved or stimulated. Indeed he
is a synthesist, even more than an analyst, in
his high discourse on spiritual themes. We
too are learning to see more clearly that the

[1] See, for instance, Professor Moberly's admirable
book: *Reason and Religion*. Longmans, Green & Co.,
1896.

mind, the I, is a unity and a whole, — that
there is will in thought and feeling, and each
in volition.   Reading his pages with this in
mind we are impressed anew with the force-
fulness, the fearlessness, at times with the
comprehensiveness of his appeals to reason,
with the fact that reason was his gift and
sphere, and that he is more than a reasoner.
In the independence of New England theologians, in their reliance upon truth, and on
modes of presenting it that cultivate thought
and increase intelligence, the influence of
Edwards has been marked.   May we never
fall away from his standard, nor trust less
fearlessly the power of truth, nor fail of
courage, nor wait less humbly and persever-
ingly at the gates of Wisdom.

I can but glance at other aspects in which
he appears as a Witness to spiritual life.

III. *He believed in its triumph.*   One
may almost say he saw it.   In the power and
grace of the Holy Spirit manifested to him
in various communities in which he preached,
he discerned the reality and promise of an
Influence by which human society can be
transformed.   This glowing hope was con-

tagious.   It has been a mighty power in our
spiritual history.

IV. *He united Faith and Practical
Piety, Religion and Morality, the Gift and
Presence of the Spirit with Training and
Discipline.*

There have been marked stages in the history of Christian life.   The first we may
characterize as spontaneous, designating thus
its distinctive note.   The primitive churches
were comparatively unformed.   Creeds, litur-
gies, governments were at most in their be-
ginnings ; but there was a Presence of God,
the gift of the Spirit, the constraining
love of a crucified and glorified Lord.   The
church looked for his speedy return.   Instead it was set to battling with a hostile
world.   It formed its creeds, consolidated
its authority, became a schoolmaster of the
nations.   The Christian life was a discipline,
— fruitful beyond measure, but less and
less a gospel.

Luther brought this gospel in again, and
wrote as its symbol, " The Freedom of the
Christian Man."

But the new principle — new by recovery
and in reception — could not at once make

itself a home, even in Protestantism. Neither could any merely external authority longer suffice. Its inadequacy has become increasingly apparent. What next? Especially as respects religious beliefs, moral training, spiritual discipline, social well-being?

Has not Edwards, our greatest spiritual seer, something to say to us? See how he conjoined with spiritual life the most searching and comprehensive "Resolutions;" how he preached justification by faith and also prepared, and led his church to adopt, the most thorough-going covenant of good works on record; and how, in his last days, he endeavored to sum up all virtue in the one comprehensive principle of Love.

What has he to give us as a watchword? Is it not, " Walk in the Spirit and bear the fruit of the Spirit; Unite a life from God, by the Spirit of God, and having the glory of God as its End, with a spiritual training and discipline in all goodness; Living faith and Christian education " ?

There is a familiar story of trembling boatmen appalled at the waves, and that one on the vessel arose and calmed them with the words : *Why do you fear? You carry*

Cæsar. As one of many storm-tossed mariners, troubled at times as to how our church is faring, I thank you for this commemorative tablet. It means — does it not? — something more than a *return* to Edwards; rather, a *going on* with him; and that still we have him with us, and will continue to have, — *him*, the noblest Roman of us all.

THE SIGNIFICANCE OF EDWARDS TO-DAY

BY REV. GEORGE A. GORDON, D. D.

THE SIGNIFICANCE OF EDWARDS
TO-DAY

In reading the Platonic Dialogues or the Divine Comedy, one is inevitably impressed with the masses of obsolete thought lying side by side with other masses full of living beauty and of permanent worth. It is as if the ancient castle were built into the mansion of to-day. In the case of Plato and of Dante the modern mind has long ago adjusted itself to this mixture of the useful and the useless. It is taken for granted that Plato as a whole, that Dante as a whole, is no longer credible; that the weeds of error press the living thought on every hand; that much must be disregarded on the way to what is precious and enduring. It would be the surest way to secure the dethronement of these kings in the realm of intellect to insist that they shall rule, not only in virtue of the exceeding brightness of the light that is in them, but also on account of the darkness in their works. Every thinker, every writer elected

to permanent influence over mankind must
die to live. The transient and perishable in
him must be set aside, his false or imperfect
interests must be disregarded, his failures in
insight and in sympathy must be noted in
order that through the precious residuum of
wisdom and of power he may continue to
civilize and bless the world. It is owing to
this criticism of love that the works of Plato
continue to be one of the great symbols of
philosophy; it is because of this same dis-
crimination that to-day Dante sings his mystic unfathomable song to a vaster audience
than at any previous time since his voice first
broke upon Europe.

This sifting process must be applied to
Edwards. As a whole, Edwards is incredible, impossible. He is nearly as much in the
wrong as he is in the right. He carries his
vast treasure in the earthen vessel of radical
inconsistency and fundamental error. No
single treatise of Edwards can to-day com-
mend itself in its entirety to the free and
informed mind. In his treatment of the
Will, the Religious Affections, the Nature
of Virtue, the History of Redemption, God's
Final End in Creation, the scheme and pro-

cess of salvation, the Christian church cannot follow him as a whole, and those who
insist upon all or none do their best to make
it none.   Only wise criticism, large and gen-
erous interpretation, the careful winnowing
of the chaff from the wheat, the clear dis-
crimination of the precious and imperishable
in Edwards from the worthless and deplor-
able, can restore him to his legitimate pre-
eminence among American theologians.

The purpose of this address is simply to
emphasize the importance of the attitude of
critical homage toward Edwards.

There may be mentioned in passing certain incidental claims of Edwards upon our
interest.   His unique genius in American
thought should not be overlooked.   In metaphysical depth and range and force he is
first and there is no second to him.   No
American thinker can be named who im-
presses one with anything like the same magnitude or quality of mental power.   Hopkins,
the younger Edwards, Emmons, and Taylor
are workers in brass compared with this
miner of gold.   They are strong mechanics;
he is an original thinker.   In originality
Bushnell is his equal, and he is far more of

an artist; but he is wanting in Edwards'
compass and depth and strength. On account of this uniqueness in our history Edwards should not be neglected. And he is
perhaps the only American intellect that deserves a place in the ranks of the world's
great thinkers. We can be sure that he is
among the kings; we cannot be sure that
another name in our whole history is there.

Nor should the surpassing strength and
beauty of his character be allowed to sink
into a mere tradition. We are not so rich
in lofty lives as to be able to ignore this passionate idealist who rose to an elevation so
uncommon and commanding. He is, first
of all, wholly sincere. "Thus many in their
affectionate pangs," he writes, "have thought
themselves willing to be damned eternally for
the glory of God. Passing affections easily
produce words, and words are cheap, and
godliness is more easily feigned in words
than in actions. Christian practice is a
costly, laborious thing. The self-denial that
is required of Christians and the narrowness
of the way that leads to life do not consist
in words but in practice. Hypocrites may
much more easily be brought to talk like

saints than to act like saints." No one can
accuse Edwards of substituting appearance
for reality or of preferring the cheap method
of words to the costly way of duty and love.
" Many hypocrites," he elsewhere says, " are
like comets that appear for a little while with
a mighty blaze, but they are very unsteady
and irregular in their motion, and are therefore called wandering stars, and their blaze
soon disappears, and they appear but once in
a great while. But the true saints are like
the fixed stars which, though they rise and
set and are often clouded, yet are steadfast
in their orb, and may truly be said to shine
with a constant light." It is not too much
to say that Edwards is one of these fixed
stars, and that he shines " with a constant
light."

Certain characteristics of Edwards' mind
relate him closely to the needs of our time.
His confidence in reason is very great, and
it should attract men to him to-day when
reasonableness is the ideal for so many be-
lievers. His confidence in metaphysical reasoning is magnificent, and it is wholly sound.
In reply to the reproach that his reasoning is
abstruse, he writes: " If the reasoning be

good, it is as frivolous to inquire what
science it is properly reduced to as what language it is delivered in, and for a man to go
about to confute the arguments of his opponent by telling him his arguments are metaphysical would be as weak as to tell him his
arguments could not be substantial because
they were written in French or in Latin.
The question is not whether what is said
be metaphysics, logic or mathematics, Latin,
French, English or Mohawk, but whether the
reasoning be good, the arguments truly con-
clusive." Wordsworth prays in his Ode to
Duty, " The confidence of reason give." It
is the prayer of the serious portion of the believing world to-day. Edwards is still one
of the high priests through whose power the
prayer may become availing.

The fundamental character of his thinking
is another point of contact between Edwards
and our needs. There should be a new edition by a competent, philosophical scholar of
the treatise on the Will. There is in this
treatise an immense mass of truth and error;
the great thinker is never wholly right, and
he is seldom altogether wrong. The treatise
is profound, acute, and comprehensive; it

might with profit be made the basis for a new and richer study of the subject, made possible by the accumulated insights of an illustrious succession of thinkers from Fichte to the teachers of philosophy to-day. The spiritual idealism of the Religious Affections puts Edwards into permanent sympathy with living Christianity. In this essay there are paragraphs of great literary excellence, pages that make one feel how rich the writer is in imaginative power. In the essay on the Nature of Virtue, which is intimately related to that on Religious Affections, we meet his ethical idealism.

Nothing is more remarkable in this work than the sentences toward the close of it, where the transformation of the natural into the ethical is recognized as the possible, and indeed the proper, life of man. " And as when natural affections have their operations mixed with the influence of virtuous bene- volence, and are directed and determined thereby, they may be called virtues, so there may be a virtuous love of parents and chil- dren, and between other near relatives, a virtuous love of our town, or country, or nation. Yea, a virtuous love between the

sexes, as there may be the influence of virtue mingled with instinct." Such words are
indeed precious. They open up the world
which belongs to man as man, the world in
which love lifts the whole animal endowment
to an ethical level, fills it with a new spirit
and stamps it with a new character.

That Edwards should see that there is no
necessary dualism between the natural man
and the spiritual, that he should note the
possible transformation of all animal instincts
and interests under the power of moral reason is indeed noteworthy ; and we should,
for the honor of Edwards, press this insight
to its fullest service. This incidental remark
about the possible transfiguration of the in-
stinctive side of human nature reappears in
his final message to his wife, as in high and
sacred consecration : " Give my kindest love
to my dear wife, and tell her that the uncommon union which has so long subsisted
between us has been of such a nature as I
trust is spiritual, and therefore will continue
forever." These remarks, by the way, may
serve to recall the many subsidiary claims of
Edwards upon the attention of the time.

The great distinction of Edwards is as a

theologian. The one supreme thing in him
that insures his permanence as a teacher is
his thought of God. What Being was to
Parmenides and Plato, what the one Substance was to Spinoza, what the Absolute was
to Hegel, God was to Edwards. He is not a
pantheist; he believes in the reality of finite
life and in the permanent reality of the human spirit. But he belongs in the front
rank of the great prophets of the Eternal;
as much as any thinker he is a child of the
Infinite.

The absoluteness of God is the heart of
Edwards' thinking. It is this that makes
him great, it is this that gives to him a high
and an enduring fascination. And this absoluteness of God for which Edwards stands,
more comprehensively and passionately, perhaps, than any other thinker in Christian
history, assumes two forms. There is what
Edwards might have called the natural absoluteness of God — He is infinite in wisdom
and in power; He has infinitely more being
than all finite things and creatures put together; He is of infinitely more consequence
than the universe which He has created. This
quantitative or physical absoluteness of God

is a constant note in the writings of Edwards.

But side by side with this quantitative or physical absoluteness of God there lies in still greater clearness His qualitative or moral absoluteness. He is infinite and wholly incomparable in righteousness, in love, and in pity. His moral being is the glory of the universe, His love an infinite excess of beauty. The saints in their utmost ecstasy fall infinitely short of the full vision of the divine beatitude. High above all vision and all rapture is the eternal loveliness. There are no words, there are no thoughts, there are no feelings adequate to the moral sublimity of the Most High. Compared with the divine truth, righteousness, love, and pity, there is in the universe, as it were, nothing but falsehood and wrong and selfishness and cruelty. So wholly transcendent is the moral excellence of God that it is as if in all worlds there were no excellence but His. This is the absoluteness of God for which Edwards stands, absoluteness of being and of excellence ; this is the great conception in the interest of which he thought and lived and wrote.

The treatise on the Will is not a disinterested psychological investigation giving rise to a disinterested philosophical generalization. That we should expect from a genuine thinker to-day. We should look for an unbiased study of mental facts and for an impartial interpretation of them. For this we look in vain in Edwards. There is, for his time, in this treatise a wonderful insight into psychological phenomena, and there is educed from this basis of fact a broad line of philosophical remark, but the purpose of the essay is something beyond that. The Arminian idea of the freedom of the will was an assertion of man at the expense of God. A self-determining will was nothing less than a limitation placed by the finite upon the Infinite. This Edwards could not endure. To break down this assertion of man at the expense of God, to remove this limitation placed by the finite upon the Infinite, to establish forever in sunlight clearness and certainty the absoluteness of God, Edwards wrote his great treatise.

It is not a purely psychological essay, it is not a strictly philosophical work, it is a tremendous polemic in behalf of Edwards' con-

ception of God, in which both psychology
and philosophy are used with gigantic vigor
and passionate persistence. The same motive is apparent in the essay on God's Final
End in Creation. It is written in the interest primarily of God and only secondarily of
man. Edwards could not glorify his God
without exhibiting Him as the redeemer and
glorifier of man. But man's good fortune
in this essay is incidental. Edwards is in-
toxicated with his vision of God, and he
leads forth nature and history, and as far as
he can the universe, as theatres for the dis-
play of the glory of God. Nowhere is the
thought of Edwards in more danger than
here. One feels how near the essay comes
to being the consecration of Infinite egoism.
Still there are not wanting saving clauses.
And even the excess of the work only serves
to emphasize what has been said, that it was
written in the interest of the absoluteness of
God.

It is unnecessary to go through in detail
other essays of Edwards. The statement
that they were written, consciously or unconsciously, by one whose supreme interest was
in an absolute God holds true of all of them.

The essay on the Nature of Virtue and that
on Religious Affections are enveloped in this
consuming theistic interest.   Predestination
becomes a joy in the hands of Edwards because it serves his conception, or seems to
serve it, so mightily.   Everywhere with Edwards God is the first consideration.   He is
the one supreme interest, and in conflict with
Him there is for this thinker no other; in
comparison with Him there is hardly any
other.   In his most characteristic moods
both of mind and heart one can hear the
great Hebrew song : —

> Whom have I in heaven but thee ?
> And there is none on earth that I desire beside thee.

The second main source of interest in Edwards is that his theology discredits his anthropology; his idea of God, his conception
of man; his views of divine perfection, his
scheme for human salvation.   A particular
scheme of salvation is a flat and fatal contradiction to the conception of the absoluteness
of God's love.   Both these ideas cannot remain permanently in the mind of the church.
If the plan of salvation includes only a part
of mankind, the God of absolute love must
be surrendered; if the God of absolute love

is at the head of the universe, the plan of
salvation inclusive only of a part of the race
must be abandoned.

At this point the importance of Edwards
for contemporary thought is of the highest.
In him, as in no other great writer, a glorious theology is brought into contradiction
with a doctrine of man which at its best is
inadequate, and which at its worst is incredible. It would be interesting to trace the
rise of Edwards' idea of man out of his idea
of God. It could be shown that for the
purposes of his doctrine of man Edwards'
doctrine of God always undergoes degradation. It might be pointed out that in his
idea of the natural or physical absoluteness
of God, when this aspect of the divine Being
is separated from His moral absoluteness,
there is the open door for the degradation
of the Edwardean theology to the level of
the Edwardean anthropology. But this endeavor cannot be continued at this time. It
is only justice to Edwards to hold him to his
best thought of God; it is only justice to
him to allow his thought of God to abolish
his thought of man. It is but the discharge
of a debt of gratitude to one of the greatest

of men to allow his thought of God to create
its own interpretation of human existence, to
give it a chance to express its inherent logic
in a new scheme of salvation.

We treat Edwards ill and not well when
we set the same value upon his worst that
we do upon his best.   We injure a mighty
character and embarrass an elemental spiritual force when we deny to Edwards' idea
of the absoluteness of God full expression in
the absoluteness of God's love for man.
Homer is read to-day with greater zest than
ever.   Nothing could be sweeter, saner or
more refreshing than his humanity as it appears in the Odyssey.   Nothing could be
much more revolting than his divinity.   The
gods of Homer have passed into mythology ;
his men and women still inherit the earth ;
they are permanent, living, heroic, and beautiful realities.   The reverse of this process
has taken place with Edwards.   Nothing
could be sublimer than his conception of God
at its best ; nothing could be more incredible
than the treatment to which he subjects the
race under God.   His theology is living,
powerful ; it is bound to become in the coming century a new and a profounder influ-

ence; his anthropology has become a mythology. His vision of absolute love abides as part of the permanent consolation of mankind; his dark and terrible inferno, like Dante's, is reduced to a symbol for a universe full of righteous love and hope as it works through woe the salvation of the sinner and the annihilation of his sin.

Edwards thus becomes the theologian of chief interest for our time. All the contradictions that work in the church to-day are in him forced into fierce antithesis. And in him, too, is the source and promise of deliverance. The questions which Edwards sets before the mind are these: Will you keep your sublime thought of God and give up your inhuman thought of man? Or will you keep your mean conception of man and degrade your high faith in God? The church is in the passionate struggle with these questions to-day over the whole land and in all denominations. The high thought about God is fighting with the unworthy thought about man. If Edwards could speak, would he not say: "Keep my best faith in God and abandon my failures to understand man. Conform not my high divin-

ity to my low humanity, but my low humanity to my high divinity. Put God on the
side of the race that He has made, and let
the race, whose friend is the Infinite, become,
through its history and hope, a new witness
for the reality of the absolute love."

Edwards is thus a providential disturber
of our unhappy peace. He is the inspirer,
in the name of his God, of a revolt against
his scheme of salvation and his whole treatment of man. He is the great abettor of a
new revolution in theology. He calls to-day
for disciples with ability and courage suffi-
cient to give consistent and complete expression to his vision of the Infinite. The stream
of his power has been diverted too long
into the impossible channels of a partialistic
scheme of human salvation; it must issue as
the river of God, full of water, and everything must live whithersoever that river
cometh. When Congregationalists and Pres-
byterians shall match the theology of Edwards with the adequate doctrine about man,
then freedom and power and peace will once
more possess their churches.

To Unitarians Edwards has a profound
message. Long ago they revolted from his

humanity; they have found the humanity which he failed to find. It is the great and enduring service of Unitarianism that it has recalled the churches of New England to the Christian view of man. But Unitarianism is uncertain in its theology, vague and ineffectual in its Christology. For the authentication of its humanity it needs the deep Christology of Edwards; for the final basis of its faith in man it needs Edwards' confidence in the absoluteness of God. Here and there, in Unitarianism, this faith in the absoluteness of God is held by runaways from the Trinitarian fold; but for Unitarianism the problem is still the problem of God. What must He be in Himself to account for humanity? What must He be in Himself to satisfy the longings with which He has filled humanity? And what is the service of Jesus Christ between the Infinite and the humanity that cries out for the Infinite? Thus to the Trinitarian, struggling to retain a false doctrine of man, Edwards presents the fresh, creative power of his conception of the Absolute Love; and to the Unitarian, fighting to keep his magnificent faith in man, Edwards offers his great faith in the God and Father of Jesus Christ.

The literal study of Edwards is disappointing and even discouraging; the logical and sympathetic study of him is rewarding and delightful. Because he is seldom wholly wrong and seldom altogether right he is hard reading. The truth in him is massive and precious, but it lies as gold lies in the rock. It must be delivered from encompassing error, set free, purified and brought to its full value through the fires of a happier experience. He is not a temple, he is a quarry. No free man of our time can live in the system of Edwards; but the material in him for building purposes is abundant and much of it is of the highest quality.

We shall expect no light from Edwards read literally, and we shall get none, in solving the Biblical problem of our generation, in making clear the identity of the reason and the Spirit of God in man, in working out our better view of human nature, in finding in humanity the supreme witness for God. Read sympathetically there is much in Edwards to help us even here. His idea of the spiritual use of the Bible places its essential value outside the scope of legitimate historical criticism, and makes it self-attest-

ing. And this is the position to which we
are coming. The Bible is full of great
voices that search the soul, and that thus
bear witness that they are from God. In
the Bible there is one Supreme voice, and
no one can add to its authority or detract
from it.

In Edwards the reason is the subject of
the operation of the Spirit, and it is easy to
see how the extension of the sphere of the
Spirit would convert all the greater products
of the natural reason into the fruits of the
Holy Spirit. There is the Edwardean conception of the spiritual man, the new creation
in Christ; clear it of its accidents, artificiali-
ties, its narrownesses and it becomes the witness for God's original purpose in mankind
to which the race is slowly lifted under the
Christian discipline of history. There is the
thought of the redeemed man as the revelation and realization of God. Nothing could
be finer than the way in which Edwards
traces this idea in his treatise on Grace,
where redeemed man is lifted into the communion of the Father and the Son and the
Holy Spirit, where the ineffable society of
the Godhead is made to express and realize

itself in redeemed human society. Make
this conception as broad and full as it should
be made, and then we shall find that Edwards is our mightiest leader in the interpretation of social man back into the social
God. The literal, the pagan, the perishable
in Edwards, has had a history long drawn
out and dismal. It is on the whole a forbidding tradition. The other side of this
great man is receiving merited recognition,
and the new theological impulse of the time
is almost certain to push to the front the imperishable Edwards.

Edwards seems to me to be a permanent
name in the world. There is that in him
which commands the attention of men.
There is in him that which is the final pledge
of permanence, the appeal to the imagination. To make this appeal it is not necessary that a writer should possess imagination.
No great writer makes less use of imagination than Aristotle, yet there is no author in
all history who makes a stronger appeal to
that power. The intellectual magnitude and
grandeur of the man constitute his everlasting fascination. A large share of this magnitude and grandeur is possessed by Edwards.

He appeals to imagination on account of his size. And besides he is one of the most imaginative of thinkers. He is an intense and a teeming idealist. His personal attitude toward the universe, his mood of devoutness and of strenuous aspiration, puts a world of light and charm into his productions. In his resolutions as a young Christian, in the glimpses that we get into the record of his spiritual life, as lover, as husband, as father, in his metaphysical polemic against the assertion of the human will at the expense of the divine will, in his profoundest thoughts upon the nature of virtue and true religion, and concerning the goal of history and the final end in creation, he is everywhere the colossal and flaming idealist.

His affinities with Dante are very great, greater, it seems to me, than to any other permanent name. He is like Dante in the story of his love, while unlike him in the fortune of that inspired passion. He is like the Florentine in the hardship and bitterness of his outward life, cast out into the wilderness as he was, and finally driven from his own New England; and he is like him in the ineffable inward consolation and peace that made all trials seem trivial and time itself as a watch in the night. The Divine Comedy and the works of Edwards have, for substance of doctrine, for the workings of imagination and passion, the play of melting pity and fierce, consuming indignation, the architecture that builds the universe into the three worlds of hopeless woe, purgatorial pain, and peace in the beatific vision, a profoundly significant relation. If we do not insist upon artistic excellence, the New England thinker and preacher is close of kin to the Florentine poet. And as Dante lives, in spite of the masses of obsolete thought that are in him, by the strength and nobleness of his imaginative appeal, Edwards will live, notwithstanding his error and imperfection, by the majesty of his appeal. His own words set forth the grounds of his permanence in the church: "The church of God has not the sun to be her light by day; nor for brightness does the moon give light to her, but the Lord is her everlasting light, and her God her glory. The new Jerusalem has no need of the sun, nor the moon; for the Lamb is the light thereof. And the ministers of Christ are, as it were, the stars that encom-

pass this glorious fountain of light to receive and reflect his beams, and to give light
to the souls of men." This glorious fountain of light is behind Edwards, and in the
mediation of it he is a fixed star, an abiding
and a beneficent servant of man.

GREETINGS

FROM YALE UNIVERSITY
BY PROF. GEORGE P. FISHER, D. D.

FROM PRINCETON UNIVERSITY
BY PROF. ALEXANDER T. ORMOND, PH. D.

GREETING FROM YALE UNIVERSITY

It gives me pleasure to bring to you the greeting of Yale. To our university nothing can be indifferent that concerns the character and fame of Edwards. His name is perhaps the foremost in the long list of her sons. He is unquestionably the most illustrious divine among the graduates of Yale. He was not only trained in the college; he also remained, after graduating, for two years, to study theology. After a short interval he came back to stay for two years more in the office of tutor. His wife, the angelic maiden whom he has portrayed in so beautiful a description, was a New Haven girl, living near the college, and the daughter of one of its founders.

Moreover, through his descendants, he has brought to the institution, in no small degree, its merit and its renown. The first President Dwight was his grandson. President Woolsey was, by a double tie of descent, the nephew of President Dwight. The

second President Dwight, who, I am happy
to say, is with us to-day, is the grandson of
the first, and so the great-great-grandson
of Edwards.   For sixty years, all but five of
them in this century, the three men just
named, surely a noble line, have presided at
Yale.

Edwards graduated in 1720, being one in
a class of nine.   Last evening I happened to
be in a group of our Japanese students.   It
brought to mind a passage in his Valedictory
Address — the original manuscript of which
I have had in my hands — wherein, even in
that " day of small things," he predicts that
the time may come when students from
foreign lands will resort to the college.
More and more, as I have returned from
time to time to the study of Edwards' writings, have I been impressed with his intellectual power and with the sanctity of his character.   It is a pity that in this country so
many of " the merely literary " — as Newman would style them — appear to know
nothing of his writings save passages in the
Enfield sermon.   They would find, if they
looked for them, in Jeremy Taylor, " the
Shakespeare of preachers," delineations of

future torment which rival the pictures of
terror in that sermon.   It is beyond question that Edwards was a theological genius
of the first order   He was, besides, an eminently holy man.   He mixed, in his soul and
in his writings, with the rigor of Calvin the
sweetness of St. Francis.   He is the Saint of
New England.

You are making a kind of reparation for
somewhat hard treatment of him in bygone
days.   In feudal times a lord would sometimes do penance by proxy, and let one of
his dependents take for him the days of fast-
ing appointed for him by the priest, or a
portion of them.   But in this case we may
safely infer from historic evidence that the
fathers of this church who made up the flock
of Edwards would heartily sympathize with
you in this proceeding to do him honor.

GREETING FROM PRINCETON UNIVERSITY

I ESTEEM it a high privilege to take part in this memorial to the extraordinary man whose presence and ministry for so many years honored this historic place and whose connection with the community and people of his love came to so regrettable an end. Now, after the lapse of a century and a half, when the passions and prejudices of the past have long since been stilled and the course of history has had time to bring into truer and larger perspective the deeds and characters of that time, it is eminently fitting that the descendants of friends and opponents of Jonathan Edwards should prove their worthiness of the great man who lived among them by uniting in this testimonial to his greatness of mind and heart and to the lasting value of his work.

It is also more fitting than any but the best informed are aware that a voice from Princeton should be included in this tribute

to Jonathan Edwards. For while Edwards'
official connection with Princeton was short
and came to an almost tragic close, it is yet
true that in an important sense Princeton
became the residuary legatee of his name and
fame. His spirit has continued to be one
of the moulding forces of the college's life.
The things in which he believed have been,
in the main, the things in which Princeton
has believed, and the type of religious life
and experience which he prized most highly
is the type that has always dominated the
religious life and history of Princeton. The
library of Edwards graces the University's
shelves ; his portrait and statue dignify and
beautify her walls, and among the presidents
of the past he holds a place as one of the
trinity of greatest names, Edwards, Witherspoon, McCosh.

Nor was there anything accidental in the
choice of Edwards as Princeton's third president. There is ample historical proof of the
fact that his relation to the new college was
almost as close as was that of its actual founders. He was in sympathy with the motives
and the course of events which brought it into
existence. He was a close friend and trusted

adviser of the group of men who were chiefly instrumental in its foundation. Many of the men who became its first trustees and all of its early presidents were his personal friends who enjoyed the advantage of his aid and counsel. He took a not unimportant part in the early financial struggles of the institution and was in complete sympathy with the motives which led its founders to incorporate religion as a coördinate element with learning in its chartered purpose. The welfare of the infant college was in truth one of the objects that lay nearest to his heart and most appealed to his interest and prayers. When, therefore, the elder Burr, the husband of his favorite daughter Esther, died, leaving the presidency vacant, it was both fitting and logical that Edwards, then little past the meridian of life, should be called to direct the destinies of the institution of which he had been so tried and true a friend.

The effect which Edwards produced on the life of Princeton is not measurable by the brief term of his presidency. He came to it in the zenith of his power and fame, and the touch of his intense personality was like the introduction of a current of electricity

into the college's life. Moreover Edwards
found his new environment in every way con-
genial. The bond that united the founders
of Princeton was to be found in their common Calvinistic faith and in the fact that they
were all actors in, or children of, the great
Religious Awakening in which Edwards took
a leading part. An important part of Princeton's constituency was Scotch and Scotch
Irish. Many of its founders and patrons
were, however, of Puritan extraction and
traced their ancestry to Old or New England.
But they were all men who had been moulded
by substantially the same traditions and who
were animated by common religious and edu-
cational ideals. Had Edwards lived to shape
the destinies of the young college for a quarter of a century it is difficult to say how po-
tent a factor in its history his genius might
have become. But even as it was, and in
view of the fact that with the advent of the
great war-president, Witherspoon, a somewhat
different but not alien tradition and other
motives arising out of the altered conditions
of the country became dominant, yet the
Edwards spirit has survived as an internal
force, conserving vital religion, stimulating

intellectual activity, holding the college true
to high ideals, and contributing to the permanence of the religious convictions of its
chartered foundation.

Princeton joins honored representatives
from other institutions in greeting Northampton to-day. She acknowledges her debt to
the great Edwards for the substance of the
faith that has been her own as well as his;
for the vital religion of the heart which his
life so well exemplified; for the pure and
consecrated character which rendered him
akin to the saints of all ages; for the strenuous life of which he is our greatest and finest
example; for that sweet graciousness of spirit
that seems all the more tender by contrast
with the sterner features of his creed.

The time is perhaps not yet ripe for a final
estimate of Edwards, either as philosopher and
theologian or as a man. There are depths in
his thought that we have not yet fathomed,
and the judgment that will do him justice
must be formed from larger and fuller data
than are yet accessible to the historian. Its
formation will doubtless involve also a measure of historic impartiality of which the present generation, in view of its nearness to the

times of partisan conflict, may not be capable.
Be this as it may, we can all unite in paying
honor to the transcendent genius and character of the man; to the marvelous subtlety
and power of his intellect; to the moral and
spiritual elevation of his life; to his unclouded
faith in God and submission to the divine
will; to his unflinching and flawless honesty
and courage; to his uncompromising devotion to the highest ideals of duty; to the un-
ruffled charitableness of his spirit and temper.

We may not subscribe to all the points of
his theology. We may not think that he has
said the last word on the freedom of the will.
We may feel that he overworks the terrors of
the law in his efforts to rouse the consciences
of men. We may think that he paints the
nature of man in colors that are too dark.
And we may entertain the fear that in the
powerful emphasis which he lays on the divine agency in religious experience, there is
danger that the agency of man will be sup-
pressed. But outside of this field of debat-
able issues there is a common ground on
which we of this generation can stand, and
from which we can pay the man an undivided
tribute. As friends of the spiritual welfare

of our country, we will agree in assigning to
Jonathan Edwards a highest rank in the gal-
axy of our religious heroes and in recognizing
him as the mightiest embodiment of spiritual
force that our country has seen.   And those
who have the best interests of our nation
at heart will not fail to see in this memorial
an omen of good for its future.   In this age,
which has been marked by such an amazing exhibition of material energy and by such
an expansion of the fields of commercial and
political enterprise, it is in the highest degree
important that the moral and religious factors
in our life should not be neglected, but that
due recognition should be given to those men
who from time to time have embodied the
great spiritual forces of our life.   In hon-
oring the man, we honor that for which he
stood ; and surely Jonathan Edwards stood for
nothing more strenuously and consistently
than for the conviction that the salvation of
a people depends on the vitality of its religion, and that a nation's material prosperity
will in the end work its ruin, if the spiritual
forces do not assert themselves in its life, and
if it fails to become fast-anchored to the rock
of a living faith in a living God.

EDWARDS IN NORTHAMPTON

BY REV. HENRY T. ROSE, D. D.

EDWARDS IN NORTHAMPTON

He was a burning and a shining light : and ye were willing for a season to rejoice in his light. — JOHN v. 35.

THE first colonists in New England were
bent on a rude and perilous experiment. It
is no marvel if there was something dark
and severe in the inheritance they left their
children. Their forbidding surroundings
matched the rigor of their enterprise. No
kindly works of men, but ungentle nature
encompassed their lives. Ardent and strenuous souls, aliens in a strange world, shut up
with the horror and pathos of their exile,
exposed to visionary dreads bred in a vast and
silent country, their loneliness, their grandeur, and their faith accumulated a tremendous spiritual inheritance for their children.
Edwards was born at a time when this herit-
age was complete. The perilous beginning
was achieved, but the stress and tension of
it were still felt. And there was as yet an
absence of the noble influence of a rich past

upon an awakening soul. There was no art
in America then, no architecture but the
rudest, no music but ragged and unmelo-
dious psalmody. But music and art and
culture were possible and sure to come, for
there was learning here, with its tastes and
ambitions. The fathers brought their clas-
sics with them. The light was dim in the
cottage windows, but it was not wasted. The
children were put at the Latin early. Edwards began it at six, and his father and his
sisters taught him. It came easily to him,
for on both sides his people were lovers of
learning and the things of the spirit.

It was hardly a quite natural boyhood, for
our judgment, which Edwards lived in the
populous home of this Connecticut pastor.
A booth was built in a very retired spot,
where he went with two other boys of his
own age for social prayer. One would like
to know the history of those other boys.
But Edwards prayed elsewhere than in this
oratory, and so far as appears, spent a blame-
less youth, without consciousness of depriva-
tion or any poverty of experience. In due
course he entered Yale College, at that period
in an ambulatory way, and was graduated,

with such honors as were then awarded, before he was seventeen. He was licensed to preach before he was nineteen, continued his study at Yale, became a tutor, and with two others of his age constituted the entire teaching force and faculty. He was invited to assume the care of a parish in New York, but declined. He was ordained and installed pastor at Northampton on the 15th of February, 1727, when he was a little more than twenty-three years of age. His marriage took place in New Haven on the 28th of July in the same year. His wife was Sarah Pierrepont, a girl of seventeen, among whose ancestors on both sides were eminent ministers. She was a woman of uncommon beauty and acquirement, attractive in manner, gifted in management, and deeply religious. In this place the eleven children of Edwards were born, one of them died here, and two were married in his house. And here he discharged the duties of his holy office for more than twenty-three years.

It was an important place to which he came, relatively, as to population and wealth, more important than it is now among the cities of the commonwealth. Nearly one

half the area of the province lay within the
borders of the county. Northampton was
the county town, to which the legal business
was brought, the local capital, and something
above the grade of a frontier settlement.
Even then it was beautiful for situation.
The friendly mountains are still the same,
the river has changed its course at one point
only. The streets follow in the main the
lines determined in the first allotment. Many
office-holders and professional men of local
distinction were settled here. Wealth was
being frugally gathered, culture and refine-
ment prevailed, and established families were
already forming the nucleus of an aristocracy.
Learning was not despised, — it never was in
New England.

When Brainerd died, his funeral "was
attended by eight of the neighboring ministers, seventeen other gentlemen of liberal
education, and a great concourse of people."
Of these seventeen thus distinguished, the
greater number were doubtless citizens of
the town.

In this proud village, rejoicing in a reputa-
tion for intelligence, the institution of most
importance was the church. There was but

one church, and it was customary to belong
to it. The church was become very large
and prosperous, and had the preëminence
among the churches outside of Boston.
Nearly all the grown people of the place
were members of the church, " beside a considerable proportion of the youth of both
sexes." The ministry of one remarkable man,
the Rev. Solomon Stoddard, continued for
thirty-seven years, " had drawn the attention
of American Christians," and achieved a certain fame in religious circles abroad.

Edwards' mother was the daughter of Mr.
Stoddard, and his coming here as the col-
league of his grandfather was a source of
family interest and hearty gratification. Delightful as the relation was, however, it im-
posed rather strenuous demands on the young
and inexperienced preacher. Mr. Stoddard
was a man of eminent gifts and prodigious
influence. He was in his eighty-fourth year
when Edwards came, closing in honor a life
of energy and action, distinguished alike for
learning and mastery of affairs. Aside from
his filial dread, Edwards' feeling for such
a man must have been one of professional
apprehension. " My grandfather," he says in

a letter to a correspondent in Scotland, " was a very great man, of strong powers of mind, of great grace and great authority, of a masterly countenance, speech, and behavior."[1] Great and masterly as he was, however, his control over his people was not entire. Neither, when Edwards came, was the seeming cordiality of his reception due to a perfect unity. The town was characterized by a great amount of the traditional New England independence. "Many of the people," says Edwards, " esteemed all Mr. Stoddard's sayings as oracles and looked upon him as a sort of deity." The officers and leaders of Northampton imitated his manners, which were dogmatic, and thought it an excellency to be like him.[2] " The people have, from the beginning," he writes, "been well instructed;" they have been "a distinguished people." But he speaks of things which had nourished " the pride of their natural temper, which had made them more difficult and unmanageable. There were some mighty contests and controversies among them in Mr. Stoddard's day, which were managed with great heat and

[1] Dwight, *Life of Edwards*, p. 463.
[2] Allen, *Jonathan Edwards*, p. 39.

violence ; some great quarrels in the church, wherein Mr. Stoddard, great as his authority was, knew not what to do with them. In one ecclesiastical controversy in Mr. Stoddard's day, wherein the church was divided into two parties, the heat of spirit was raised to such a degree that it came to hard blows. A member of one party met the head of the opposite party and assaulted him, and beat him unmercifully. In latter times, the people have had more to feed their pride. They have grown a much greater and more wealthy people than formerly, and are become more extensively famous in the world, as a people that have excelled in gifts and grace and had God extraordinarily among them, which has insensibly engendered and nourished spiritual pride. Spiritual pride is a most monstrous thing. There is great reason to think that the Northampton people have provoked God greatly against them, by trusting in their privileges and attainments." [1]

What is referred to here is the frequency of revivals in the church. Before he came, the fame of this place as a scene of great revivals had gone abroad. Five of these at least had

[1] Dwight, *op. cit.* p. 463.

occurred during Mr. Stoddard's ministry, and
the church had been greatly strengthened.
The series was continued during Mr. Edwards'
pastorate, and celebrated in his writings, until
this place became famous as the centre of the
mighty religious phenomena known in history
under the name of the Great Awakening.
"This place," said Edwards, "was preëm-
inently, in this respect, a city set on a hill.
People at a distance have been more ignorant
of our former imperfections, and have been
ready to look upon Northampton as a kind of
heaven upon earth."

But these excitements, in the nature of the
case, could be only occasional. The name
for the revival common at that time is suggestive; it was known as "an attention to religion." The intervals between the revivals
were marked by inattention. Toward the end
of one of these intervals Edwards came, and
found the spiritual and moral situation of his
parish far from satisfactory. The last revival,
less intense or extensive than some others, had
occurred nine years before. "Mr. Stoddard
was then witnessing a far more degenerate
time among his people, particularly among
the young, than ever before." Dissipation

and immorality were common. "Family government too generally failed; the Sabbath
was extensively profaned and the decorum
of the sanctuary was not unfrequently dis-
turbed." There was also a strife between
two parties in the town which led to factional
contention and disputes about public mat-
ters.

If one is amazed to learn of such dis-
orders in a Puritan church, he needs to be
reminded how intimately the town and the
church were united, so that there was no
class in the community for whose morals the
church was not held responsible. Nor may
we accept as calm, accurate representation
of fact the contemporary lamentations over
the degeneracy of the times. Yet there certainly was then in New England a decline
of religion and a grievous decay in morals,
and many prophets announced the failure of
the glorious experiment of the founders, and
the speedy coming of divine retribution upon
a cold and unfaithful church. But great
changes were impending, bringing spiritual
and moral renewal. And of these Edwards
was the most prominent leader and representative, a providential man, a man for the

hour, with the gifts and fortune of the reformer, the seer, and the martyr.

The reader of the scanty records of his life here receives the impression of something mysterious, indistinct, elusive. It was a lofty and rapt existence, apart, unearthly. His nature was so rare and fine, with its interest in things remote, unseen and holy, the detachment from earth was so complete, that his feet were as the feet of an angel when he touches the ground. The fact is almost a pathetic one, that his ordination is recorded in his own hand in the family Bible, among the births and baptisms and deaths of his children. So, without note or comment, is the incident of his dismission. Evidently he began his work in a mood of seriousness and consecration, and we shall see further on in what temper he closed it. But what of the years between? There is left a journal kept in his youth, the story of a spiritual experience so little involved with the earth, that one might fancy it the story of a soul that had missed being born. This is continued but a little while, and a very full account survives of the events which were connected with his departure from this

place; but the rest, so far as details are concerned, and adventures, is almost a blank.
It was a life of amazing industry, but all its interests were intellectual and professional.
It was the life of a scholar, meditative, solitary in a manner, self-centred, without many books, ascetic, remote, untraveled, mystical. His two companions were the intuition and the spirit. What can one make of a life like that, with its twelve or thirteen hours a day of intense study, its heavenly preoccupations and profound reveries?

Yet his Sundays were his great days, and those with his own people were his best. He attained a wide fame, for he went abroad and made a brilliant appearance now and then in another pulpit: in Boston; in Enfield with an immortal, almost sinister, effect; in Easthampton, Long Island, in the church of Dr. Buell and Lyman Beecher. His great work was done here, for he was not an evangelist, and his work was preaching rather than the cure of souls. He was not a model pastor, and except when the need was urgent he made no calls. He was wanting in the social gifts; he could not readily converse on common themes; on this side lay his great deficiency, a certain destitution in the human qualities. This is the fault in his theology and philosophy. It was a scheme without man in it, or at least a real humanity. Man is as abstract in it as is God.

One series of events diversified this great existence and brought it out of obscurity into a universal fame. Edwards' ministry was attended with notable revivals. It is not that these spiritual excitements were new phenomena here. It is said by Dwight that during eighty years the church had been favored with more numerous and more powerful revivals of religion than any church in Christendom. Nor is it that he brought an unequaled number of converts into the church. Some of his successors indeed, in shorter terms of service, received a larger yearly average of accessions. But these revivals signalize his preaching as the source of religious influences of immense extent and permanent effect. Here began the Great Awakening, and Edwards was identified with it from its beginning, its human author, its advocate, its representative. He wrote its history and its defense. He studied its phenomena, he published its triumphs, he bore witness to its practical, ethical value and saving efficiency in society. The effects of this great work were felt on the other side of the world. In New England it accomplished a moral revolution, and a most significant change in the town. In the first revival "upwards of fifty persons above forty years of age, ten above ninety, near thirty between ten and fourteen, and one of four, in the view of Mr. Edwards became the subjects of the renewing grace of God."[1] Large numbers of converts were received into the church; at one time it numbered about six hundred and twenty members, including almost the entire adult population. And these persons, with other subjects of grace "in the county of Hampshire, near the banks of the river Connecticut, were turned from a formal, cold, and careless profession of Christianity to the lively exercise of every Christian grace, and the powerful practice of our holy religion."[2]

These effects, resulting in the religious and moral uplift of New England, bear witness to the marvelous power of Edwards as a preacher. It was his habit to set forth in most unsparing terms the darker as-

[1] Dwight, *op. cit.* p. 123.   [2] *Ibid.* p. 137.

pects of what he thought the truth. But it must not be supposed that he preached nothing else so willingly as the rigors of the law, the depravity of the heart, and the doom of sin. He did not shun these themes, and when they were chosen his method was one of unmitigated thoroughness. His preaching dealt in terms of his own time. It appealed to motives almost dormant now; it moved the souls of men with terrors which seem to us almost fantastic. His preaching had its terrific aspects. He emphasized as dark and merciless the wrath to come. He brought his hearers sometimes to agonies of apprehension. The tumult of distress at Enfield, once the token of his marvelous power, has been remembered to his reproach.

He deserves a kinder recollection. These were not the only themes for his discourse, and not the favorite ones. The greater number of his published discourses are of another type. They breathe even yet a passionate tenderness. They are full of exhortation, entreaty, charity. It is not that he delights in cruelty, when he is setting forth the awful forecasts incident to his theology. There is an infinite sorrow and a great pity

in his heart. His vigorous logic led him
on those burning paths. But he did not
love that zone of fire and terror. More
often his preaching is qualified by a marvelous intellectual light, by dignity, grace, a
holy submission, a patience and compassion
truly Christlike. It is not fair to judge him
from two or three sermons — and those un-
read — or from two or three phrases, which
it is more probable he never uttered.

It was his manner also which helped to
make him what he is confessed to have been,
the greatest preacher of his age. Is there
any emergence here of an element due to his
Welsh ancestry? His gift was individual,
original; he was neither made nor spoiled by
the schools. He was inimitable, his power
was never described. He was no stormy
orator. He spoke quietly and with little
gesture, but as one who knew. His eyes
were seeing things of which he talked, and
not the people to whom he spoke. He was
calm and pale, he had the form of an ascetic; rapt and serious in look, it was his
habit to lean upon the pulpit with marvelous
eyes alight, a face illuminate from within,
earnest, confident, authoritative, with nothing

in his vesture or manner priestly except that his heart was touched with the feeling of our infirmities.

This is the man so rare and noble, the greatest preacher of his time, whose name shed lustre on the church and town, who at the full summit of his power, after nearly a quarter of a century of service, was turned out of his office ungraciously. Love and aid and confidence were his due from these people, most of whom were his spiritual children. Reproach and ingratitude and derision were heaped upon him. How shall we account for the painful estrangement of the hearts of his people?

The causes lie far back and beneath the surface. At his coming he was received with seeming unanimity. But there were discontented ones, and rivalries. Ten years after his coming there were signs of disaffection. "At that time," he says, "while I was greatly reproached for defending the doctrine of justification in the pulpit, and just upon my suffering a very open abuse for it, God's work wonderfully broke forth among us." The great revival quenched these murmurings. But it is evident that he had to do

with a restless people. Mrs. Edwards' journal betrays occasional apprehensions. No
doubt there were years of quiet when the
pastor's popularity seemed very great. The
church was proud of him, but pride hardly
constitutes an enduring bond. At length
arose the famous case of discipline involving
so many of the young people in the practice
of reading forbidden books. It has been
suggested by Leslie Stephen that these books
were some of the popular novels of Richard-
son.[1] But this can hardly be, for a few
years later Edwards himself read Sir Charles
Grandison " with deep interest, regarding it
as wholly favorable to good morals and purity
of character." [2]

No doubt there was a graver offense than
this in the parish, but possibly the inquiry
was not conducted in the discreetest manner.
There followed a great decline in Edwards'
influence and popularity. The discontent
grew ominous when he declared his position
in reference to the qualifications for communion at the Lord's table. " I know not,"

---

[1] *Hours in a Library*, ii. p. 63, quoted by Allen, *op. cit.*
p. 259.

[2] Dwight, *op. cit.* p. 601.

he wrote, more than a year before the event, "but this affair will issue in a separation between me and my people."

In establishing their theocratic government in New England, the founders made church membership a requisite for citizenship. There came a relaxation in practice, and, in a sort of associate relation by means of the Halfway Covenant, many men were entitled to vote and hold office. This arrangement at first did not admit these partial members to the Lord's Supper. Here, however, Mr. Stoddard made a radical innovation, and welcomed to the communion baptized persons who presented no evidence of conversion. He taught, and his example was widely followed in these parts, that the Lord's Supper was a channel of converting grace. This high sacramentarian view Edwards distrusted from the beginning, and after years of study became convinced that he must refuse the sacrament to those who would not make a confession of religion. The practice of later years has vindicated Edwards in this matter. There is not now a single church in our order that accepts Mr. Stoddard's position, or retains the Halfway Covenant. But in that time it was believed by many that Edwards' position was revolutionary, dangerous, and extreme. Many of his people were personally affronted as though their own standing in the church and social respectability were affected by it. The church was convulsed with the dispute. In four years not a single person applied for the privilege of communion. Then, when a candidate appeared and refused to meet Mr. Edwards' conditions, which were far less rigorous as to credal statements than many forms of admission now in vogue, the quarrel broke bounds, and his dismission followed.

This in the briefest form is the story as it has come down to us. But possibly with another story the issue might have been the same. He was a great, lonely spirit, remote from the common life, unappreciated by most of the people. Many were irritated by his spirituality, his cold and saintly demeanor. He was too great for parochial estimation. Possibly, also, he was deficient in the saving grace of tact as he was in humor. And he was the victim of a popular excitement. He was caught in one of those deliriums which had prevailed in the parish at intervals. Only it was not a religious revival this time, it was a popular frenzy, a contagious excitement of zeal, cruelty, injustice, breaking all restraint of reason and sanity.

It was a grievous trial for Edwards, borne in a manly and Christlike temper. His was not the common sorrow attending on the breaking up of a relation expected from the outset to be temporary. Long pastorates were the custom, and it was anticipated that the pastoral office should be held for life. If not, there was reproach attached to the minister, or at least suspicion. Many circumstances made it a very bitter experience for a man of proud and sensitive nature to be dismissed from his church with so many signs of impatience and disrespect. But throughout the whole affair the bearing of Edwards was dignified, noble, admirable. In the conduct of his case, in letters, journals, writings, addresses, in his incomparable farewell sermon, there is no petulance, anger, vindictive passion. Just as little is there any affectation of long-suffering, or ostentatious forgiveness of enemies. He does not pose as a martyr. He does not strive, or cry, or cause his voice to be heard in the streets. There is amazement more often when his people turn against him. It is a manly sorrow. He does not conceal his sense of injury, but there is nothing weak or mean or vengeful in his mood. There is no retraction, arrogance, upbraiding. His last word is a message marvelous for self-control, full of peace, counsel, conciliation, so admirable in its spirit, Christlike, tender, that it is in our hearts as we read to revere and love the man.

It has been suggested lately, perhaps with too much confidence, that the town and church alike have been insensible to the value and glory of Edwards' work and life, and slow to make due reparation for an ancient wrong. But it is not our greater fault that we have not before this reared a fitting monument to his memory. We do him more grievous wrong when we ignore the beauty and charm and dignity of his character, the splendor and breadth of his personality. Some of us have had for him a certain esteem and pity due to the prejudice of ignorance. We think him possessed of a dark, brooding and irritable temper. We imagine that he thought of God as an infinite despot, cruel, insatiable, delighting in suffering, and ordaining eternal awards after the arbitrary counsel of His will. And we have fancied that the terrors of his system were reflected in his own sombre spirit, so that in his life he was morose, gloomy, and cold, dispensing chill and shadow as he moved, and that his heart and home and church were full of gloom. There is no truth in it. It is true that he was an ascetic, but he was that from a glad and happy choice because he preferred to live in the spirit. He was a mystic, and his meditations were profound and unworldly, searching the deep things of God. Though his manners were severe and dignified after the custom of the age, his mind was alert and his heart was rich in feeling. He was no fearsome soul, plagued with apprehensive terrors. In many points no two men present greater contrasts than Edwards and Matthew Arnold. But we are reminded of the modern stylist, critic and maker of phrases when we come so often on Edwards' favorite words *sweet* and *bright*. One who delights in such words and their meanings, not merely as formularies, cannot be of a cheerless habit. His life was an excellent, high, sweet passage in the sombre music of those days. There were intervals of darkness and sorrow, but his vision of God was on the whole to an astonishing degree clear and bright. Early his mind took its bent and kept it, and he held with a glorious and happy constancy to the majestic, strong truths in which he first believed. These are his own words : " God's absolute sovereignty and justice with respect to salvation is what my mind seems to rest assured of, as much as of anything that I see with my eyes ; at least it is so at times. But I have often, since that first conviction, had quite another sense of God's sovereignty than I had then. I have often had not only a conviction, but a delightful conviction. The doctrine has often appeared exceedingly pleasant, bright, and sweet."

THE EARLY IDEALISM OF EDWARDS

BY H. NORMAN GARDINER

THE EARLY IDEALISM OF EDWARDS

THE history of philosophy in America attracts but little notice from those who treat of the general history of philosophy. It is hardly considered even by ourselves. And indeed it must be confessed that America has hitherto had but little direct influence on the main currents of the world's speculative thought. In this department of the spiritual life we have been more imitative than creative. Nevertheless the history of philosophy in America is nothing to be ashamed of and it contains at least one great name. Competent critics unite in regarding Jonathan Edwards as the most original metaphysician and subtle reasoner that America has produced, while there is not wanting authority for pronouncing him not only the greatest of American thinkers, but "the highest speculative genius of the eighteenth century." [1]

[1] A. M. Fairbairn in his essay on Edwards in *Prophets of the Christian Faith*. Cf. Moses Coit Tyler, *Hist. of Am. Lit.*, ii. p. 177 ; A. C. Fraser, *Life of Berkeley*, p. 182.

Until recently Edwards has been best
known as a philosophical theologian by his
treatise on the Will. This work is still
spoken of as " the one large contribution
which America has made to the deeper phil-
osophic thought of the world." [1] Now, however, there is a tendency to qualify somewhat
the admiration formerly expressed for this
great work, and to emphasize rather the importance of such writings as the Treatise on
the Religious Affections, the Observations
on the Nature of Virtue, and the Treatise
on God's Chief End in Creation, while the
key to Edwards' thought, his theology, his
preaching, and in a manner the very type
of his piety, is sought in the undeveloped essays of his youth.[2] These essays he himself
never published. His biographer, Sereno
E. Dwight, first published the notes on The
Mind and on Natural Science in an appendix to his Memoir of the theologian in

[1] Quoted by A. V. G. Allen, *Jonathan Edwards*, p. 283.

[2] This is the point of view from which Allen's work on
Edwards is written. But see especially the notable article
by Prof. Egbert C. Smyth, " Jonathan Edwards' Idealism,"
in *The Am. Journ. of Theol.*, Oct., 1897, pp. 950 ff. Cf. also
the same author's " Some Early Writings of Jonathan Edwards " in *Proceedings of Am. Antiq. Soc.*, Oct., 1895.

1829. The Miscellanies, containing observations on topics of divinity, exist still for
the most part only in manuscript.[1] It is
generally known that the two series of notes
first mentioned contain an expression of idealism akin to, if not identical with, that of
Berkeley, though it is not generally understood precisely what the relation is. Strangely
enough, Edwards never once certainly alludes
to his early view of the material universe in
any of his finished writings. And yet it can
be shown, I think, both that the conception
was with him an original expression of personal insight, and that there is no reason to
suppose that he ever abandoned it; that in
short it was no mere accidental product of
youthful fancy, or echo of another's teaching,
but was intimately connected with the deepest and most permanent elements of his speculation. I propose therefore to call attention
once more to these still little regarded writings of Edwards, and to attempt at least a
general estimate of their significance.

[1] The *Miscellanies*, containing over 1400 numbers, were
continued through life, but some of them appear to be con-
temporaneous with the other notes mentioned, to which they
allude. A fourth series of notes, on the Scriptures, does
not here concern us.

As bearing on the question of originality,
it is not without importance that Edwards
intended by these notes on The Mind and
on Natural Science to prepare two great
treatises embracing the whole mental and
material universe. On the outside of the
cover containing the notes on Natural Science were written hints on the arrangement
of the work, and on the inside a longer list
of rules to be followed in its composition.
Among the latter, the following are perhaps
worth citing as characteristic of the author's
intellectual straightforwardness : "Try not
to silence, but to gain ; " "Not to insert any
disputable thing, or that will be likely to be
disputed by learned men ; for I may depend
upon it, they will receive nothing but what
is undeniable from me, that is, in things exceedingly beyond the ordinary way of thinking ; " "In the course of reasoning, not to
pretend anything to be more certain than
any one will plainly see it is, by such expressions as — It is certain — It is undeniable —
etc. ; " "Let much modesty be seen in the
style."[1]   There are two series of things to
be considered or written about, one of thirty-

[1] Dwight, *Memoir of Edwards*, p. 702.

three, the other of eighty-eight numbers, among which lists the notes proper are interspersed. Besides these, there is an introduction on the Prejudices of the Imagination, followed by three propositions and seven postulates dealing with conceptions of general physics. Finally, there are two essays separate from the rest, one a highly theoretical discussion of atoms, the other, of the greatest importance for our purpose, a metaphysical discussion Of Being. The notes throughout are full of accurate observation and acute reasoning, containing more than one anticipation of later discoveries, and showing plainly that if Edwards had devoted himself under favorable circumstances to scientific pursuits, he would have attained in them the highest distinction.[1]

The series of notes on The Mind begins with the full title of the proposed work, namely, The Natural History of the Mental World: being a Particular Enquiry into the Nature of the Human Mind with respect to both its Faculties — the Understanding and the Will — and its various Instincts and Active and Passive Powers.[2] Following this

[1] See Moses Coit Tyler, *op. cit.* pp. 185 f.
[2] The modern reader will not be misled by the designa-

is a brief sketch of an introduction explaining the distinction between the external and internal worlds, and showing the importance of the latter as an object of study. Then comes an enumeration of the topics to be treated, the fifty-six mentioned being evidently nothing but memoranda jotted down at intervals as they happened to occur to the writer.

Many of these topics are extremely interesting, not only as showing the kind of subjects with which Edwards' mind was at this time occupied, but also as indicating his attitude on certain important questions. I will mention a few of them to illustrate. Among those of a logical character, we note one on the nature of judgment, proposing to show

tion Natural History into expecting a genetic, or even an exclusively descriptive, treatment of the subject-matter ; these aspects are included, but the philosophical interest is predominant, as it is in Locke's " historical, plain method," as it is — to go back to the origin of the term — in Aristotle's definition of psychology as ἡ τῆς ψυχῆς ἱστορία, the natural history of the soul. Edwards conceives of the scope of his work in the spirit of the older writers rather than in that of Locke, and it is perhaps not without significance that he should have recognized thus early the claims of the active side of our nature to parallel treatment with the cognitive.

that judgment differs from the mere mental
presence of ideas, and is hence not the perception of the agreement or disagreement
of ideas. Edwards is here getting beyond
Locke's definition in the direction of more
modern doctrine. In another topic we have
a certain anticipation of Hume in the recognition of a twofold ground of assurance, the
law of contradiction, and the law of causal
connection. The former is still regarded, as
universally before Kant, as the principle of
mathematical demonstration, but the latter is
held to be entirely distinct and irreducible.
Among the psychological topics, we note the
significantly large number which directly or
indirectly treat of the affections and the will.
I find no less than twenty-two relating to
these subjects, considerably more than a third
of the whole. We note too such topics as
the following : the nature of the sensation a
man has when he almost thinks of a thing ;
whether the mind perceives more than one
object at a time ; how far the mind may perceive without adverting to what it perceives,
and similarly of the will ; how far all acts of
the mind are from sensation ; whether there
could have been any such thing as thought

without external ideas ; how far imagination is involved in thought. The subject of imitation is suggested. Edwards is much impressed by the effect of example and desires to study its influence on opinion, taste and fashion, and why it is that at one time a vogue lasts an age, while at other times it is of short duration. He had unusual opportunity for the investigation of this subject later, at the time of the Great Awakening, and he has, in fact, left us a work, in his narrative of that movement, which is rich in material for the student of social suggestion; but its significance, in this respect, though not wholly ignored, was little considered at the time by himself. One of the most noteworthy of the purely psychological topics treats of the connection of ideas. Locke had recognized only one principle, custom ; Edwards, as later Hume, distinguishes three, association of ideas — evidently Locke's custom — resemblance, and cause and effect, and all three processes he speaks of in quite mechanical fashion as a kind of mutual attraction and adhesion of ideas.[1]

[1] It may not perhaps be superfluous to remark in passing that Locke's view is really nearer to the modern doc-

Strangely enough, very few of the numbers have to do directly with ethical matter except in relation to other topics; indeed, strictly speaking, there is perhaps only one, that concerning the proper foundation of blame. On the other hand, there are at least four which treat of the sense and influence of beauty.[1]

Of the more properly metaphysical questions, we observe with special interest the following : " In how many respects the very being of created things depends on laws, or stated methods, fixed by God, of events

trine ; it not only recognizes a single principle but a physiological, explaining all association as due to "trains of motion in the animal spirits, which once set going, continue in the same steps they have been used to, which by often treading are worn into a smooth path." Only Locke had apparently no idea of the different points of view from which the effects of these "trains of motion " could be regarded, and from which Hume reduced them all to custom again. The differences had long ago been recognized by Aristotle, but Edwards had almost certainly no knowledge of the fact.

[1] In the notes which follow the enumeration of topics to be treated, the subject of excellency is the first to be discussed and is also among the last ; under this head we have the outline of a philosophical theory of æsthetics. The discussion of this topic fills over eight pages, more than a fifth of the space occupied by the entire series of notes.

following one another;" and again, "the
manifest analogy between the nature of the
human soul and the nature of other things
. . . how it is laws that constitute all permanent being in created things, both corporeal
and spiritual." In these and other numbers
we have a clear indication of the author's
idealism; the language here used suggests
even the more modern formula, that the essence of things is constituted by relations.
But the point of special note is that Edwards
intended to base his whole treatise on metaphysics. In the topic numbered 8, he tells
us that the positive exposition of the nature
of the human mind was to be preceded by a
discussion concerning Being in general, with
the object of showing to what extent the
nature of entity determines human nature.[1]

The notes proper follow the enumeration
of the topics to be treated. And the relation between the two is a very free one —
they by no means correspond either in order
or in subject. Thus of the fifty-six topics
in the programme, I find twenty-one which
are not discussed in the notes directly at all,
while of the rest the discussion is in part

[1] Dwight, *op. cit.* pp. 664 ff.

fragmentary, and in large part in other connections and from different points of view from those originally suggested. On the other hand, I find at least ten of the seventy-two numbers of the notes treating of topics not mentioned in the original list at all.

In his theory of knowledge Edwards recognizes in no uncertain way both the fact and the importance of the sensational element. He holds that " all our ideas begin from sensation, and that without sensation or some other way equivalent wherein the mind is wholly passive in receiving ideas, there could never be any idea, thought, or act of the mind." So essential does it seem to him that the mind should have data furnished it to work on that he suggests that the first ideas even of the angels must be of some such kind as those we receive from the affection of our senses. Sensational elements enter into the higher processes of thought and reasoning, and the ordinary sequence of thought depends on the mechanical association of ideas. At the same time, he holds that in its capacity for reflection, the mind has power to actively deal with its data, and to contemplate things spiritual (59). And

not only is it active, but it contains its own
principles of action.   One of these principles is being : it is an absolute necessity that
something should be.   Another is causality :
whenever we see anything that begins to be,
we intuitively know that there is a cause for
it (54).   A third is the principle of the final
cause (54).   These principles must be held
to interpret and limit what was said above
on the mechanism of ideas.

An interesting feature in this general discussion is the treatment of universals.[1]   Edwards rejects the nominalist view on the
ground that deaf and dumb persons, and not
only those who use language, abstract and
distribute things into kinds.   At one time,
following Locke, he seems to consider all
such distribution as arbitrary.   But in later
numbers he holds that many of our universal
ideas are not arbitrary, but have their foundation as well in the order of nature and the
constitution of our minds as in the circumstances and necessities of life.   Indeed, " the
foundation of the most considerable species
or sorts in which things are ranked is,"
he says, " the order of the world — the

[1] Dwight, *op. cit.* pp. 683 ff.

designed distribution of God and nature."
This order is what constitutes the real essence of things. Edwards, therefore, by no
means agrees with Locke in identifying real
essence with nominal essence. With this
doctrine of universals agrees his doctrine of
truth.[1] He vacillates in his language, defin-
ing truth now as the perception of the relations between ideas, and now as the agreement of our ideas with existence ; but strictly
speaking, he says, truth is the consistency
and agreement of our ideas with the ideas of
God ; it consists not merely in the perception of the relation of ideas, but in their
adequateness. We here rise to the conception of a higher kind of universality than
that contemplated in the ordinary doctrine
of abstract ideas, the conception, namely, of
the universality of a divine order in the
world. It is here that the doctrine of real
essence first gets metaphysical significance.
And with this we have reached once more
the subject of Edwards' idealism.

The idealistic doctrine is variously expressed and defended in the notes on The
Mind, particularly in the articles entitled

[1] *Ibid.* pp. 687 f.

Existence, Substance, and Excellence; also in the article Of Being in the notes on Natural Science. This last is a curiously interesting document, and there is good reason for regarding it as the first of the series setting forth the idealistic view.[1] As Edwards seems to allude to it more than once in other of his notes,[2] and as the question of its date has some bearing on the originality of the conception, I venture to give a somewhat full analysis of its contents.

It begins by discussing the absurdity of attempting to conceive a state of absolute nonentity. Such an attempt, says Edwards, puts the mind into mere convulsion and confusion; it is the greatest contradiction and aggregate of all contradictions. "If any

[1] One reason for this supposition is that early in the notes on The Mind (9) Edwards speaks of having already observed that space is a necessary being, and yet as having also shown that all existence is mental. There is nothing of this in preceding numbers, but it is found in the essay on Being. That this essay is among the most youthful of Edwards' writings is obvious. See Smyth, *Some Early Writings*, etc., where the point is argued in detail.

[2] *E. g.*, Obs. 6 in the *Miscellanies*: "We have shown and demonstrated . . . that no matter is substance but only God." Obs. 27a : "We have shown that absolute nothing is the essence of all contradictions." See Smyth's article cited above in *Am. J. of Theol.*, p. 953.

man thinks that he can think well enough how there should be nothing, I 'll engage that what he means by nothing is as much something as anything he ever thought of in his life." To get a complete idea of nothing, he says later, " we must think of the same that the sleeping rocks dream of." But if it is impossible to think absolute non-being, then it is necessary that some being should eternally be, and this necessary and eternal being must be infinite and omnipresent. Such a being is space, and space is God. Nor would any one " stick at " this assertion, were it not for the gross conceptions that we have of space.[1] " And how doth it grate upon the mind," continues Edwards, after further insisting on the necessity of being, " that something should be from

---

[1] The idea that space is God, or an attribute of God, is said to be Cabbalistic. Spinoza's view is well known. The doctrine has some affinity with Newton's conception of absolute space as the *sensorium* of God, but it was expressly denied by Newton's disciple Clarke, who teaches rather that space is an *immensum* " caused by " and an " immediate and necessary consequence " of God's existence (*Works*, ed. 1723, iv. pp. 608, 624), and was rejected by Berkeley as pernicious and absurd (*Pr.*, § 117). Edwards could hardly have expressed himself as he did had he at this time been acquainted with Berkeley's view.

all eternity and nothing all the while be conscious of it . . . yea, it is really impossible it should be that anything should be and nothing know it." This is the idealism: all existence is existence for consciousness. " Then you 'll say, if it be so, it is because nothing has any existence anywhere else but in consciousness. No, certainly," he replies, " nowhere else but either in created or uncreated consciousness." He then proceeds to elucidate the conception. He first supposes a world of senseless bodies known only to God ; but what sort of a being could such a world have other than in the divine consciousness ? To the objection that on the same grounds a room in which there was no finite mind would only exist in the mind of God, he replies that created beings are conscious of the effects of what is in the room, but that otherwise there is nothing in a room shut up but only in God's consciousness. " How can anything be there any other way ? " he asks, adding that this will evidently appear to any one who thinks of it with the whole united strength of his mind. It is only our imagination that leads us to suppose the contrary. Suppose the world devoid of light and motion. If there were no light, there would be no color; and if there were no motion, there would be no resistance, and so no solidity, and if no solidity, then no extension, figure, or magnitude. What, then, is to become of the universe? The inference is that, apart from sense-experience, a universe can exist nowhere but in the mind of God. The whole concludes with the corollary that only those beings which have knowledge and consciousness are properly real and substantial.[1]

The impression conveyed by even this mutilated account of the essay is unmistakably one, I think, of youthful ardor and mental independence. The thesis is stated with a positiveness, an assurance of conviction, quite out of proportion to the strength of the argument. A mature thinker would have been both more cautious and more logical, especially a thinker of Edwards' calibre. In the treatise on the Will we have a closely reasoned argument meeting the objector point by point. Here we have the bold assertion of an intuition that has taken possession of a mind metaphysically predisposed,

[1] Dwight, *op. cit.* pp. 706 ff.

but the grounds and difficulties of which have
not yet been fully thought out. And this
impression of youthfulness is greatly en-
hanced by a perusal of the whole article,
especially in the form in which it has recently
been printed from the original manuscript
with all its absence of punctuation, its bad
spelling, and its misuse of small letters and
capitals.[1] Professor Smyth, to whom we are
indebted for this reëditing, has made it well-
nigh certain from a careful comparison of the
MSS. of Edwards' early writings, that this
essay on Being was written when Edwards
was still a sophomore in Yale College.

The other articles mentioned show more
maturity, and serve to bring out the idealistic
view in greater fullness. Thus in the article
on Existence, having first shown that the
objects of vision are mental, " since all these
things, with all their modes, do exist in a
looking-glass," the author proceeds to argue
that the resistance which still remains to
body is equally, with its modes, solidity, figure, and motion, dependent on mind. This
last line of argument is worked out still more
completely in the article on Substance.

[1] E. C. Smyth, *Some Early Writings*, etc. pp. 33 ff.

The point is first made that the essence of bodily existence is solidity. Take away solidity and nothing is left but empty space. It is then contended that solidity or impenetrability is as much action, or the immediate result of action, as gravity. We attribute the falling of bodies to the earth to the influence of a force; why not attribute their coming to rest to a like power? But it is entirely from such phenomena as this that we get the idea of solid body. Our experience, according to Edwards, is as follows: We receive from certain parts of space ideas of light and color, and certain other sensations by the sense of feeling; and we observe that the places whence we receive these sensations are successively different. We also observe that the parts of space from whence we receive these sensations resist and stop other bodies, and again that bodies previously at rest exist after contact in different successive parts of space; and these observations are according to certain stated rules. "I appeal," says Edwards, "to any one who takes notice and asks himself, whether this be not all that ever he experienced in the world whereby he got these ideas; and that this is all we have or can have any idea of in relation to bodies." But if body in our experience is nothing but this, then what we call the substance of the body must be a power or agency, and there is nothing in the nature of the thing itself to cause it, when set in motion, to stop at such limits rather than at any others. Edwards concludes that this agency is intelligent and voluntary.[1]

Like other idealists, Edwards is at great pains to defend his view of the material universe from misunderstanding. It is not meant, he explains, that the world is contained in the narrow compass of the brain; the brain itself exists only mentally, as other things do, and its place is only an idea like other places. Therefore things are truly in those places in which we find them to be. Nor is this view inconsistent with physical science. For to find out the reasons of things in natural philosophy is only to find out the proportion of God's acting; and the case is the same as to such proportion whether we suppose the world only mental or otherwise. Nor again is it necessary to make use of any other than the common terms in

[1] Dwight, *op. cit.* pp. 674 ff.

speaking of things. For although in the absence of human perceptions material things exist only in the divine mind, yet the effects of God's acting are in every case just as if things had continued to exist in finite minds. And although ideas of sensation depend on the organs of the body, and the organs of the body have only a mental existence, still it is not proper to say that those ideas depend only on other of our ideas; for the organs of the body exist in the divine mind even when they have no actual existence in finite minds. Indeed, Edwards goes so far as to reject as wholly misleading the statement that bodies do not exist without the mind; for within and without, he says, are spatial terms and space relations are themselves mental. The doctrine that the material universe exists only in the mind means that it is absolutely dependent on the mind for its existence. In another note he explains more fully why and how material things must be supposed to exist in the divine mind when they have no existence in created minds. The explanation rests on the assumption that the order of nature is fixed. Things are so connected that were anything other than it is the whole universe would be different. Hence the existence of anything not actually existing in ideas in finite minds consists in God's supposing of them in order to render complete the series of things as eternally conceived by Him; and this supposing is nothing but God's acting in the course and series of his exciting ideas as if the things supposed were in actual existence in our experience. At the end of this note Edwards quotes Cudworth's account of Plato's subterranean cave, indicating that he considered sensible things as shadows and ectypes of the divinely conceived order.[1] His own most adequate statement of his idealism is in the following noteworthy passage : " That which truly is the substance of all bodies is the infinitely exact and precise and perfectly stable Idea in God's mind, together with His stable Will that the same shall gradually be communicated to us and to other minds according to certain fixed and exact established methods and laws ; or, in somewhat different language, the infinitely exact and precise divine Idea, together with an answerable, perfectly exact, precise and stable Will with

[1] Dwight, *op. cit.* pp. 669 ff.

respect to correspondent communications to created minds, and effects on their mind." [1]

Such in brief outline is Edwards' idealism as it appears in these early and loosely connected notes. The conception is not worked out, and the expression is in places crude; but the theory as a whole is penetrating and profound, and the reasoning at times astonishingly acute. We have now to consider two questions which may contribute towards a just estimate of its significance. The first is : Where did Edwards get these ideas? And the second : What was their influence on his own later thinking ?

The answer at once suggested to the first question is, from Berkeley. All readers have been struck by the resemblance between the views of the young American thinker and those of his elder British contemporary. Fraser calls Edwards " an able defender of Berkeley's great philosophical conception ; " he and Samuel Johnson, he says, " adopted " and " professed " Berkeley's philosophy.[2] Professor Fisher, of Yale, also calls Edwards

[1] *Ibid.* p. 674.
[2] Fraser, *Life of Berkeley,* pp. 182–190 ; his ed. of *Berkeley's Principles,* p. xviii.

a Berkeleyan.[1]   Georges Lyon, in treating of
Edwards in his work on English Idealism in
the eighteenth century,[2] declares that the dependence on Berkeley is unmistakable.   He
even undertakes to point this out in some
detail.   He quotes, *e. g.*, the following:
" The ideas we have by the sense of feeling
are as much mere ideas as those we have by
the sense of seeing," remarking that this is
precisely the position whereby Berkeley in
his Principles did away with what was equi-
vocal in his Theory of Vision.   He refers
to Edwards' argument for the merely mental existence of all the objects of vision,
because, namely, " all these things . . . do
exist in a looking-glass," as almost a phrase
of Berkeley's, and at any rate one of his
favorite proofs.   He also considers the argument to be similar to Berkeley's in which
Edwards maintains the unlikeness between
our ideas of space and those which a man
born blind would have.

All the evidence for this alleged influence
of Berkeley is entirely internal.   There is no

---

[1] G. P. Fisher, *Discussions in History and Theology*, p. 229.
[2] Georges Lyon, *L'Idéalisme en Angleterre au XVIIIe
Siècle*, ch. x.

external evidence that is worth considering. Fraser suggested that Edwards may have become acquainted with Berkeley's philosophy through Samuel Johnson, who was tutor at Yale between 1716 and 1719, while Edwards was a student. This suggestion, about which much has been plausibly argued on both sides, has lately been pretty definitely refuted from Johnson's own manuscript, entitled " A Catalogue of Books read by me from year to year since I left Yale Colledge." The record begins with the year 1719–20. There is no mention of anything of Berkeley's before 1727–28. In that year and the year following the Principles are entered, and in 1729–30 the Dialogues and the Theory of Visions.[1]

[1] We are indebted for this piece of evidence, as for so much else relating to Edwards' early philosophy, to Professor Egbert C. Smyth, who publishes it in a note in the *Proceedings of the American Antiquarian Society*, x. p. 251, 1897. In the same note he demolishes the suggestion of Johnson's biographer Beardsley that the " new philosophy " against which the students were warned when Johnson graduated in 1714 was Berkeley's. Beardsley says that at that time something had been heard at Yale of the great names of Descartes, Boyle, Locke, and Newton, " as well as of a new philosophy that was attracting attention in England," but against which the young men were warned. An earlier biographer, Chandler, had stated the matter

We may dismiss then the view that Edwards was made acquainted with the Berkeleyan theory by Johnson. It is probable that Johnson himself first learned of it when he went to England for episcopal ordination in 1723. But may not Edwards have read Berkeley? This is possible as far as the dates go, for Berkeley's Principles were published in 1710, his Dialogues in 1713. From four to seven years, therefore, elapsed between the publication of Berkeley's early

---

differently : " the students had heard of a new and strange philosophy that was in vogue in England, and the names of Descartes, Boyle, Locke, and Newton had reached them, but they were not suffered to think that any valuable improvements were to be expected from philosophical innovations." This suggests the writers mentioned as the authors of the "new philosophy." Dr. Smyth's publication of the original of these statements from the MSS. of Johnson's autobiography makes this certain. Johnson says that when, in 1714, he took his degree, the students at Yale had heard "of a new philosophy that of late was all in vogue, and of such names as Descartes, Boyle, Locke, and Newton, but they were cautioned against thinking anything of them, because the new philosophy, it was said, would soon bring in a new Divinity and corrupt the pure Religion of the Country." A comparison of Johnson with his biographers Chandler and Beardsley affords a good illustration of the facility with which, under rapid compilation, historical facts can get perverted. Cf. Smyth, *Some Early Writings*, etc. p. 26.

philosophy and the earliest date claimed for these writings of Edwards. Against this, however, must be set the opinion of the late President Porter that there is no evidence that any of these works were known at Yale College when Edwards was a student, and that there is reason to believe that they were not then accessible.[1] This opinion is confirmed by a letter of Berkeley's to Johnson dated from Newport the 25th of June, 1729, in which the writer does not know whether, even so late as then, his disciple possesses a copy of his Principles, and expresses his intention of sending him one.[2] It is more than likely, to be sure, that many of these notes of Edwards were written after graduation in the years of his tutorship. Indeed, there is positive evidence from a note in his diary that as late as February 12, 1725, he was still meditating on these problems. But considerations of this sort, which allow more time for the acquaintance with Berkeley, are

[1] Porter, *The Two Hundredth Birthday of Bishop George Berkeley*, etc. p. 71.

[2] Quoted by Smyth, *Some Early Writings*, etc. p. 25. Fraser, *Life of Berkeley*, p. 174, says that the *Principles* had early fallen into Johnson's hands, but he does not say how early, nor does he cite any authority.

offset by the evidence for the very early date of the essay Of Being, which already contains the idealism.

We are thus thrown back on the internal evidence and on general probability. Lyon finds the view that these notes on The Mind and on Natural Science were the original work of a college student utterly incredible. If they were, he says, then Edwards would have united in himself the genius of several Pascals and have surpassed by far in intellectual gifts Galileo and Newton combined. This exaggerates the claims actually made for him. No one maintains that he invented all this physics and metaphysics out of whole cloth, that he reproduced nothing of what he read or heard, that he owed nothing to others for stimulus and suggestion. Nor is it necessary to assume that all the notes were written before he graduated. Still it would be remarkable if a mere boy of fourteen or fifteen should have arrived independently, even allowing for outside suggestion, at an idealistic conception of the material universe, even a crude one. But Edwards was a remarkable boy. Already at the age of ten he had composed a curious and somewhat humorous little tract on the immateriality of the soul. Lyon considers this, to be sure, a mere echo. Possibly. The same, however, can hardly be said of his paper on the flying spider, written when he was about twelve, " a child," he calls himself in the letter introducing it. This boy's paper on the flying spiders combines the most careful personal observations of these insects with the most acute scientific reasoning and hypothesis, and is surely one of the rarest specimens of precocious scientific genius on record.[1] Just before his thirteenth birthday he entered Yale College, and the next year, at the age of fourteen, he read Locke's Essay on the Human Understanding, enjoying, as he tells us, in the perusal of its pages, a far higher pleasure " than the most greedy miser finds, when gathering up handfuls of silver and gold from some newly discovered treasure." In view of this extraordinary precocity of his mental development, and the undoubted in-

[1] The paper on the *Flying Spider* was published by Dwight, *op. cit.* pp. 23 ff. But see, especially, the article on it, with facsimile reproductions of the MS., by Professor E. C. Smyth, *Andover Review*, xiii. pp. 1–19.

dependence, vigor, and originality of his mind, there is nothing incredible in supposing that he arrived at his idealism under similar influences to those which affected Berkeley. There is no improbability in believing that he reached this conception while still an undergraduate, and that he expressed it at first crudely in the article on Being, and afterwards more adequately as the idea unfolded in his mind. Berkeley himself, we remember, began the Common-place Book, containing the material for his Theory of Vision and his Principles shortly after taking his first degree at the age of nineteen. Edwards graduated at seventeen, and there is every reason for believing that his intellectual powers, at no time inferior to Berkeley's, matured much earlier than the latter's. Moreover, he had been brought up from earliest childhood in an atmosphere of theological conceptions highly stimulating to a temperament so naturally — one might almost say so preternaturally — reflective, and so eagerly and profoundly speculative.

But however it may be with the precise date of the article on Being, there are strong and to my mind convincing indications in

the notes themselves that Edwards was not
dependent for his idealism on Berkeley.
In the first place there is no mention of
Berkeley's name. To be sure, Edwards is
not given to the mention of other writers,
being much more interested in the exposition of his own ideas. Throughout the
two series of notes on The Mind and on
Natural Science, the only authors referred
to by name are Cudworth, Newton, Locke,
Hobbes, and Ptolemy. But as Professor
Fisher observes, " Edwards was not the man
to conceal a real obligation." [1] Dr. Smyth
cites an instance of his candor in this respect
in his remark at the end of a brief note
on Density Pores, " N. B. This has been
thought of before." [2] But no one can read
Berkeley without a vivid sense of the novelty
and originality of his thinking. The young
student who had read Berkeley must surely
have felt himself under a real obligation.
But there is nothing whatever of this in
Edwards. On the contrary, there is evident
consciousness of independence. He is pre-
paring, as we have seen, to write a book in

[1] Fisher, *op. cit.* p. 234.
[2] Smyth, *Some Early Writings*, etc. p. 24.

which these views of his will be given to the
world. He is aware of their novelty. He
is careful, therefore, to guard himself against
misapprehension, especially in the matter of
the seeming denial of the existence of bodies
outside the mind. " It is from hence I
expect the greatest opposition," he writes.
This, I take it, is an expression of a sense of
personal ownership in his ideas.

Moreover, if Edwards had derived his
idealism from Berkeley, we should expect a
much more direct reflection of Berkeley's
thought and language. How, for instance,
could he have written as he did on the subject of universals if he had been acquainted
with Berkeley's vigorous polemic against the
doctrine of abstract ideas? No ideas are
more characteristic and oft-repeated in the
early works of Berkeley than the following :
the impossibility of perceiving distance by
sight, the arbitrariness of God in connecting
ideas of sight and ideas of touch, the influence of suggestion — a peculiarly Berkeleyan
word — in perception, the objects of sight a
divine visual language. Is it conceivable or
to be regarded as a mere accident that a
young student, reproducing ideas derived

from the reading of Berkeley, should have
given no hint of being affected by such all-
pervading and altogether fascinating conceptions? But they are entirely absent from
these notes of Jonathan Edwards. In comparison with this negative evidence, the paral-
lelisms of language and argument cited by
Lyon appear trivial. How could any idealist
fail to observe that ideas of touch are as much
ideas as those of sight? And what more
natural illustration of the ideality of objects
of vision than their reflection in a looking-
glass? Or what more likely an observation
than the difference between a blind man's
ideas of space and ours? This last, moreover, he could have got, and probably did
get, from Locke.

But we can go further. Not only is there
no proof that Edwards derived his idealism
from Berkeley, but it is clearly evident that
his idealism has, to say the least, a different
accent and character from that of the author of the Principles of Human Knowledge
and the Dialogues of Hylas and Philonous.
Berkeley's early doctrine is, as every one
knows, that the *esse* of material things consists in their *percipi*. Now it is no doubt

true that in urging this doctrine his main
object was to establish the reality of the
divine being and action, and the substantial-
ity and causality of spirit. That spirit is
alone substantial and causal is indeed the
real Berkeleyan idealism. But the relation
of things sensible to spirits, and especially to
the mind of God, is hardly considered by
Berkeley in his early writings; he contents
himself with the thought that God imprints
the ideas of material things on our senses in
a fixed order. To the objection that material things when not actually perceived by us
must be non-existent, he can only reply that
"there may be some other spirit that perceives them, though we do not."[1] The *esse*
of things is thus their *percipi*. Later in life
Berkeley went beyond this, and taught that
the *esse* of things is not their *percipi*, but
their *concipi*, that the world in its deepest
truth is a divine order eternally existing in
the mind of God. But it is this doctrine
which, along with the phenomenalism which
he shares with Berkeley, is the characteristic
doctrine of Jonathan Edwards. It is implied
in his conception of the real, as distinguished

---

[1] *Principles*, § 48.

from the nominal, essence, and in his conception of truth as the agreement of our ideas with the ideas of God, and it is definitely expressed in various passages, best perhaps in the formulation of his idealism already quoted : " That which truly is the substance of all bodies is the infinitely exact and precise and stable Idea in God's mind, together with His stable Will that the same shall gradually be communicated to us and to other minds according to certain fixed and established methods and laws." The phenomenalism in Edwards is relatively subordinate. But similar ideas are not at all prominent in Berkeley before the Siris, which was not published till 1744.

If now, discarding the hypothesis of Berkeleyan influence, we raise the question as to where Edwards got the suggestions for his idealism, I am inclined to answer, Mainly from three sources : from Locke with his doctrine of ideas; from Newton with his doctrine of colors ; and from Cudworth with his diffused Platonism. These authors we know he read. If we go beyond these, I would as soon include hypothetically Descartes with the problematical idealism of the early part of the

Meditationes, or John Norris, whose Theory
of the Ideal or Intelligible World, published
in 1701, reproduced ideas of Malebranche,
which, as Lyon has pointed out, are star-
tlingly paralleled in some of these notes of
Edwards, as I would include Berkeley, whose
doctrine was itself developed under similar
influences. The fact is, idealism was, so to
say, in the air, and in Arthur Collier we
have a contemporary illustration, if we may
believe his account of himself, of a similar
independent development of idealistic doctrine to that which we here claim for Edwards. Collier's book[1] was not published
indeed till 1713, but he adopted, he tells us,
his new thought concerning the meaning of
sensible existence as early as 1703. He was
then twenty-three ; Berkeley at twenty-five
published the Principles six years later.

[1] *Clavis Universalis: or a New Enquiry after Truth.
Being a Demonstration of the Non-Existence, or Impossibility,
of an External World.* The author nevertheless held
strongly to the existence of a material world " numerically
different from every material world perceived by mere creatures," namely, " the great mundane idea of created matter
. . . by which the great God gives sensations to all His thinking creatures and by which things that are not are preserved
and ordered as if they were." (Reprint of 1837, p. 7.)
This is strikingly analogous to the thought of Edwards.

The question still remaining, namely, as to the effect of this early idealism on Edwards' later thought, is more difficult to answer in detail, and it can only be touched on here with the greatest brevity. As already indicated, the formal expression of the doctrine, so far as it relates to the material world, is strangely absent from the later theological treatises. There is a suggestion of such an expression in a passage cited by Dr. Fisher,[1] from the treatise on Original Sin, where it is said that late improvements in philosophy have demonstrated the course of nature to be nothing but the established order of the agency and operation of the author of nature ; but this view is not necessarily idealism, for, as Edwards tells us, it was also held by his opponent Taylor. There is, however, another passage in the same treatise cited by Dr. Smyth [2] which has a decidedly idealistic complexion, Edwards observing " that all dependent existence whatsoever is in a constant flux . . . renewed every moment as the colors of bodies are every moment by the light

[1] Fisher, *op. cit.* p. 231.

[2] Smyth, "Jonathan Edwards' Idealism," *Am. Journ. of Theol.*, Oct., 1897, p. 956.

that shines upon them; and all is constantly proceeding from God, as light from the sun." This is perhaps the nearest approach to a restatement of the earlier view in the theological treatises that can be found. But there is evidence that Edwards continued his reflections along the lines struck out in the youthful essay Of Being, and that its fundamental thought influenced him profoundly. It recurs, for instance, in a number of the notes in the Miscellanies with probable allusions to that essay. In the note in the diary of the 12th of February, 1725, to which reference has been made, Edwards writes that what he now wants is as clear a knowledge of the manner of God's exerting Himself with respect to spirit and mind as he has of his operations concerning matter and bodies. Dr. Smyth cites from the MS. of the Miscellanies a number of passages which show Edwards at work on this problem, endeavoring to apply the idealistic conception to the relation of God's mind to finite minds. Thus "Man's reason and conscience seems to be a participation of the divine essence" (210): "An inclination is nothing but God's influencing the soul according to a certain law of nature"

(301): God comprehends the " entity of all
His creatures, . . . they are but communications from Him : communications of being are
not creations of being " (697). In Obs. 267
he finds the existence of God implied in the
mere coming to pass of a new thought in the
creature. He further applies his idealism to
the more specific theological doctrines. Thus
in the following passage cited by Dr. Smyth,
he applies it to the doctrine of the Trinity :—

I will frame my reasoning thus : If nothing has
any existence at all but in some consciousness or idea
or other; and therefore the things that are in us created consciousness have no existence but in the divine
idea ; or, supposing the things in this room were in the
idea of none but of God, they would have existence no
other way, as we have shown in the natural philosophy,
and if the things in this room would nevertheless be
real things ; then God's idea, being a perfect idea, is
really the thing itself ; and if so, and all God's ideas
are only the one idea of Himself, as has been shown,
then God's idea must be His essence itself, it must be
a substantial idea, having all the perfection of the substance perfectly ; so that by God's reflecting on Himself the Deity is begotten : there is a substantial Image
of God begotten.[1]

[1] Obs. 94. Smyth, *l. c.* p. 954. Cf. Obs. 179 : " It the
more confirms me in it that the perfect idea God has of Himself is truly and perfectly God, that the existence of corporeal things is only ideas."

His view of the union of the two natures in the person of Christ is also colored by his conception of a universe constituted of divine ideas and their intercommunications.[1]

In a charming little tract on the Excellency of Christ, which Professor Smyth first published from the MS. in 1880,[2] Edwards expatiates on the visible world as a reflection of the glory of Christ's divine attributes: the flowery meads and gentle breezes are emanations or adumbrations of His benevolence; the fragrant rose and lily, of His love and purity; the green trees and fields and the singing of birds, of His infinite joy and benignity; and similarly of other aspects of natural beauty. "There are also many things," he continues, "wherein we may behold His awful majesty; in the sun in his strength; in comets; in thunder; in the hovering thunder-clouds; in ragged rocks, and the brows of mountains." Nor is all this, as it may perhaps at first appear to us, purely fantastic. There is a profound philosophical thought underlying it, the same, namely,

[1] Smyth, *l. c.* p. 962.

[2] In an appendix to his edition of Edwards' *Observations concerning the Scripture Economy of the Trinity.*

as that of Plato in his conception of the
visible world as an image or shadow of the
eternal Ideas.   Here the thought takes on a
theological coloring from its connection with
the doctrine of Christ as the creative Logos.
" Now we have shown," writes Edwards, in
introducing these reflections, " that the Son
of God created the world for this very end,
to communicate Himself in an image of His
own excellency.   He communicates Himself
properly only to spirits, and they only are
capable of being proper images of His excellency, for they only are proper *beings,* as we
have shown.   Yet He communicates a sort of
glimpse of His excellencies to bodies, which,
as we have shown, are but the shadows of
beings, and not real beings."   Where has he
shown this ?   Nowhere, so far as we know,
but in those early notes on The Mind and
on Natural Science.   The document fits in
with the other notes on Excellency, though
having a more theological cast of expression.
If we may judge from its place in the series
of observations in the Miscellanies, the
160th, and assume with Dwight that the
first 150 belong to the two years preceding
and the two following Edwards' graduation,

we shall not be wrong in finding in it an allusion to those other series of notes. But while there are indications in the note on Excellence of the thought here expressed concerning the relation of Christ to creation, it is to one of the latest of Edwards' works that we must go for its elaboration. The Dissertation concerning the End for which God created the World has for its entire subject this very theme. This work, posthumously published, may justly be regarded as the most boldly speculative work in English in the eighteenth century. The very title, as Dr. Allen remarks, "suggests the profound and fascinating speculations of Gnostic theosophies." The subject is so lofty that Edwards himself confesses its obscurity and the imperfection of the expressions used concerning it. Nevertheless, he essays to discuss it in the pure light of reason, and the result is a work comparable only to the works of the great speculative mystics. The central thought of the treatise is this, that there is in God a disposition, as an original property of His nature, to an emanation of His own infinite fullness, and that it was this disposition which excited Him to create the world, and so that the emanation itself was the last end which God aimed at in the creation. This being so, the creation itself tends to appear as an emanation. Indeed, this is the language which Edwards constantly uses in speaking of it, being doubtless unaware of the associations and implications of the word. " The old phrases," says Dr. Allen, " such as the overflow of the divine fullness, diffusion of the divine essence, emanation from God compared with the light and heat which go forth from the sun, these constitute the verbal signs of Edwards' thought." To be sure, where he uses these phrases, he refers more particularly to the spiritual creation, and there is no direct suggestion in any part of the treatise of the early phenomenalistic view of matter. But the whole trend of the thought is towards a comprehensive idealism which makes God all in all.[1]

This was, indeed, the whole trend of Edwards' thought throughout. His mind is steeped in the contemplation of the perfection and absoluteness of God. He conceives of God as the absolutely sovereign Reason,

[1] See A. V. G. Allen, *Jonathan Edwards*, pp. 327 ff.

loving supremely His own infinite perfections and the creature so far as it manifested and reflected them, creating the world for this sole purpose, and governing it according to His sovereign pleasure. In the early note on Excellence, it is argued that God, being Infinite Being, all other being must necessarily be considered as nothing, that, " in metaphysical strictness and propriety, He is and there is no other." In the latest of the treatises, the whole system of created beings is spoken of " as the light dust of the balance (which is taken no notice of by him that weighs), and as less than nothing and vanity." Relatively to God, man has no power : he is an elect vessel either of His beneficent grace or else of His retributive justice. The language of the Calvinistic theologian concerning decrees is only the reflection and investiture of the deeper thought of the speculative philosopher that God's activity is from and to Himself — an uninterrupted exercise of glorious will. In harmony with these views, Edwards' type of piety is thoroughly the mystic type, the enjoyment of God in complete self-surrender to His spirit. And God communicates Himself to spirits directly by an immediate illumination. This is the theme of one of Edwards' most remarkable sermons.

Now this conception of God is what underlies his conception of the ideality of the material universe. It is not that the phenomenalism brings with it the idealism : it is the deeper idealism of the thought of God which brings in the phenomenalism. It is not necessary, therefore, that we should look for precise expressions in the later works of the early view. As Edwards himself said in the notes on The Mind : " Though we suppose that the existence of the whole material universe is absolutely dependent on Idea, yet we may speak in the old way, and as properly and as truly as ever." And it is in the old way that he speaks, in the main, in the works by which he is best known. But the early metaphysics blends with the later theology ; its spirit pervades it ; and it is scarcely to be doubted that had Edwards been asked at any time in his later years to state exactly what he thought of the constitution of the material universe, he would have replied in much the terms in which he had expressed the meditations of his youth, that its substance was the "infinitely exact and precise divine Idea, together with an answerable, perfectly exact and stable Will, with respect to correspondent communications to created minds, and effects on their minds."

APPENDIX

APPENDIX

To complete the record of the Edwards Celebration in Northampton the following additional documents are here inserted by way of appendix.

I

PRAYER BY THE REV. PETER McMILLAN, PASTOR OF THE EDWARDS CHURCH

We bow before Thy throne, O Thou Sovereign Lord of all, in deepest gratitude for the incarnate love and wisdom of Jesus Christ our Lord, and for His spirit of truth and righteousness abroad in the earth.

May the messages brought to us at this time be of the truth and character of Jesus Christ, as reflected in Thy servant, who so long ago ministered holy things in this place ; whose pure and holy life attracts us here ; whose patience and gentleness rebuke our rebellious pride, and whose steadfast gaze into the deep things of God shames our complaining glances at Thy truth.

We bless Thee that there lingers here the sweetness of so rare a spirit, even as the fragrance of a bruised flower ; that his strong faith in the Eternal God steadied many a soul in the hour of darkness and of inner conflict, until the day broke and shadows fled away ; that to multitudes he has seemed the simple, serene, strong man of God.

May all our hearts be as living tablets — memorials
— whereon shall be written our devotion to Thee, O
Christ; our gratitude to the prophets who foretold Thy
coming, and to apostles who proclaimed Thee Redeemer
and Lord; to the martyrs of every age who have taught
us heroism and self-sacrifice in devotion to truth and
duty; to the uncounted hosts through whom has come
to us the rich legacy of faith and hope and love.

We ask all in the name of Him, who — however the
hearts and minds of men may change from age to age
— is the same yesterday, to-day, and forever, Jesus our
Prophet and Priest, the King of men.   Amen.

II

ADDRESS OF WELCOME BY THE REV. DR. HENRY T. ROSE

FATHERS AND BRETHREN, — The First Church of
Christ in Northampton, organized in 1661, extends to
all of you a hearty welcome to these commemorative
services. It is an especial honor that so many eminent
scholars, professors in colleges and schools of theology,
have felt so deep an interest in the occasion as to con-
sent, in a crowded time, to visit this place and take
part in our happy observances. We greet also with
sincere pleasure the pastors and messengers of the
ancient churches whose representatives composed the
council which met on this ground a hundred and fifty
years ago, Friday, the 22d of June, 1750, and pronounced the dissolution of the pastoral relation between
Jonathan Edwards and this church. Of the ten churches
invited to that council many are represented here

IN MEMORY OF
JONATHAN EDWARDS
MINISTER OF NORTHAMPTON
FROM FEBRUARY 15 1722 TO JUNE 22 1750
THE LAW OF TRUTH WAS IN HIS MOUTH AND
UNRIGHTEOUSNESS WAS NOT FOUND IN HIS LIPS
HE WALKED WITH ME IN PEACE AND UPRIGHTNESS
AND DID TURN MANY AWAY FROM INIQUITY MAL 2 6

to-night. And besides these the church in Stockbridge, to which Edwards went as missionary after leaving Northampton, has sent its representative. Here I need say no more, except to express the hope that the quiet decorations about the pulpit may seem to be in harmony with the hour. The laurel may remind us of Edwards' love of nature, and the boughs of green are from the elm which, according to tradition, was planted by his hands.

III

REPORT AND PRESENTATION ADDRESS BY THE CHAIRMAN OF THE MEMORIAL COMMITTEE

The Committee entrusted with the erection in this church of a memorial to Jonathan Edwards was appointed by the parish in December, 1897, and was added to in December, 1899. Two of the gentlemen so appointed were unable to serve, two who contributed for a time valued aid in knowledge and interest have died. The five members remaining make the following report.[1]

The principal work of the committee has been to decide on the general character of the Memorial, to select the artist and coöperate with him in the elaboration and execution of the design, to raise the necessary funds, and to arrange for the present service. In Mr. Herbert Adams the committee found a sculptor not only technically competent, but rarely sympathetic in

[1] Mr. J. R. Trumbull, the historian of Northampton, and Rev. Joseph H. Twitchell, D. D., died; the other members were Miss E. O. Baker, Mrs. Wm. G. Bassett, Miss M. A. Jordan, Miss Kate Tyler, and the chairman, H. N. Gardiner.

appreciation of his subject, and with a refined sense of its artistic possibilities. In harmony with the place and the occasion, he has represented Mr. Edwards as if preaching, as the minister of Northampton. The pose of the figure is, we think, dignified and graceful. The features were modeled on the original portrait of 1740, but express perhaps more benignity and indicate a richer experience. "I have tried," Mr. Adams writes, "to show a man who believed and felt most sincerely and deeply — one who had tried, and would still try, to teach those things which he believed to be true and vital. At the same time, it seems to me that such an intense and earnest nature must have felt somewhat discouraged and sad that all could not believe as he did, particularly so during the last of his stay in Northampton." After this, it will not be surprising if one detects in the presentment a suggestion of the preacher of the Farewell Sermon rather than the prophet of the Great Awakening. In the main, however, the representation is that of the character set forth in the inscription underneath, the divine eulogy of an ancient minister, fitly, as we think, appropriated here: "The law of truth was in his mouth, and unrighteousness was not found in his lips: he walked with me in peace and uprightness, and did turn many away from iniquity."

All the money required for the expenses of the Memorial has been raised, about half of it from persons and organizations connected with this church and parish, including the Sunday School, the Junior Endeavor Society, and the First Church Guild. The remainder came from other persons in town and from abroad, several contributions being received from England. Among the contributions most highly esteemed may be mentioned a lecture by Mr. George W. Cable, the novelist, on February 15, the anniversary of Edwards' ordination here, and the gifts of money from the Edwards Church of this city, from the Old South Church in Boston, and from the living descendants of the theologian. The Memorial, therefore, represents more than the desire of this church to atone for the past; it represents rather a general sentiment of respect for the illustrious minister who belongs to no single church exclusively, but to the historic Church Universal.

I have also to announce two gifts unrecorded in our contribution list, but greatly to be valued: first, the services of the distinguished gentlemen who for the honor they bear to the genius and character of Jonathan Edwards freely unite with us in rendering this tardy tribute of justice to his memory, and who by their words and presence are helping to make this service historic; secondly, the gift of an autograph letter written in Northampton in 1740 by Mr. Edwards to the Rev. Eleazar Wheelock, afterwards president of Dartmouth College. This letter, which refers to the approaching visit of Mr. Whitefield to Northampton, is hereby presented to the town, to be preserved in the Forbes Library, by Dr. Wheelock's great-great-granddaughter, Miss Sarah A. Hopkins. I venture to express the hope that Miss Hopkins' wise example will prompt others who may possess similar precious documents to place them in this or some other public library, where they will be securely kept and made permanently available.

And now, thanking all who have contributed in any way to the completion of this enterprise, in their behalf and in the name of the committee I hand over to the assessors of the parish, to be kept by them and their successors in trust for the parish, the church, the town, indeed for all who may anywhere be interested in our great traditions, the Jonathan Edwards Memorial Tablet; and I have the honor to ask Mr. Charles Atwood Edwards, the theologian's great-great-grandson and the oldest living representative of the line of descent from Jonathan Edwards the younger, to unveil the tablet — to the glory of God, and in perpetual memory of his servant, dismissed from the pastorate of this church a hundred and fifty years ago to-day, and to-day recognized the world over as one of the greatest of theologians, the most impressive of preachers, and the saintliest of men.